PALESTINE
FOR THE
THIRD TIME

Jews of Poland

Series Editor: Antony Polonsky (Brandeis University)

PALESTINE
FOR THE
THIRD TIME

Ksawery Pruszyński

Translated and with an introduction
by Wiesiek Powaga
Foreword by Antony Polonsky

Boston
2020

Library of Congress Cataloging-in-Publication Data

Names: Pruszyński, Ksawery, 1907-1950, author. | Powaga, Wiesiek, 1958- translator, writer of introduction. | Polonsky, Antony, writer of foreword.

Title: Palestine for the third time / Ksawery Pruszyński ; translated with an introduction by Wiesiek Powaga ; foreword by Antony Polonsky.

Other titles: Palestyna po raz trzeci. English | Jews of Poland.

Description:
Boston, MA : Academic Studies Press, 2020. | Series: Jews of Poland

Identifiers: LCCN 2020030464 (print) | LCCN 2020030465 (ebook) | ISBN 9781644694770 (hardback) | ISBN 9781644694787 (adobe pdf) | ISBN 9781644694794 (epub)

Subjects: LCSH: Pruszyński, Ksawery, 1907-1950--Travel--Palestine. | Authors, Polish--20th century--Travel. | Palestine--Description and travel.

Classification: LCC DS107.3 .P813 2020 (print) | LCC DS107.3 (ebook) | DDC 956.94/04--dc23

LC record available at https://lccn.loc.gov/2020030464
LC ebook record available at https://lccn.loc.gov/2020030465

ISBN 9781644694770 (hardback); ISBN 9781644695654 (paperback)

ISBN 9781644694787 (adobe pdf); ISBN 9781644694794 (epub)

Book design by Kryon Publishing Services (P) Ltd.
Illustrations remastering by Anna Carson. Cover design by Ivan Grave

Published by Academic Studies Press
1577 Beacon St.
Brookline, MA 02446

press@academicstudiespress.com
www.academicstudiespress.com

Przyjacielowi z ławy uniwersyteckiej

MOJŻESZOWI POMERANZOWI

ofiarowuję

"I dedicate this book to my
university friend—MOJŻESZ POMERANZ"

Contents

Foreword:
Ksawery Pruszyński

We, Polish people, have special reasons to promote the State of Israel. We have fought for too long time for a state of our own not to understand such a fight, when undertaken by others. We know unfortunately better than many other nations what it means for a nation to have a state of its own. Our nation knows the gas chambers like the Jewish people did and our nation has not forgotten, like some others, the sad lesson of this war.

—Ksawery Pruszyński, speech delivered at the UN as chairman of the United Nations Subcommittee Number One on Palestine in November 1947[1]

In his relatively brief life, Ksawery Pruszyński (December 4, 1907–June 13, 1950) embodied the tragic fate of Poland in the first half of the twentieth century. He was born into a noble family near the village of Wolica Kierekieszyna (today Volytsya-Kerekeshyna) on the Zbrucz River in southern Volhynia (Ukraine). The founder of the village was a Tartar, Kierekiesza, and the area was characterized by its mixture of religions and ethnicities. As Pruszyński himself put it:

I came into the world at a crossroad of worlds and times, cultures and beliefs, languages and races, classes and nations, on a snowy December day in a blizzard, when a sleigh was sent for the Jewish "barber"—the doctor was already there, but courtesy required the presence of the barber.[2]

---

1   This speech is reproduced as it was delivered in Pruszyński's characteristic English.
2   Quoted in Józef Hen, *Nie boję się bezsennych nocy* (Czytelnik: Warzsawa, 2001), 23.

This area, part of Tim Snyder's "Bloodlands," saw considerable violence in the twentieth century. When Pruszyński was barely three, his father Edward was killed, probably in a clash with a horse thief. His mother Anna was a member of a magnate family, the Chodkiewiczes, who had fallen on difficult times, which was why they were willing for her to marry Edward, who was thirty-five years her senior.[3] She was now responsible, on her own, for bringing up her two sons, Ksawery and his younger brother Mieczysław.

In 1918, during the Russian Civil War, Anna was forced to flee the area with her sons and settle, in somewhat impoverished circumstances, in Kraków; there, and with her family's help, she was able to support herself by giving French lessons. After the Treaty of Riga, which ended the Polish-Soviet war, all the Pruszyński properties were located within the Soviet Union. Pruszyński always had a powerful sense of being a "boy from the Kresy" and clearly greatly missed his lost "little homeland." When he served in the Polish consulate in Kiev in 1933–1934, he went illegally to Wolica Kierekieszyna, only to find that nothing remained of his family's wooden manor house. He was certainly very conscious of his roots. As he told Józef Hen, a Polish Jewish writer with whom he became friendly in the Soviet Union during the war, what inspired all his writing was "[a]bove all the fact that the past of the Rzeczpospolita [pre-partition Poland-Lithuania] was our past."[4]

Pruszyński completed the first part of his secondary education in Żytomierz and continued it at the Jesuit school in Chyrów (now in Ukraine), near Przemyśl, one of the most prestigious in Poland. He then studied law at Jagiellonian University, specializing in medieval German law under a leading conservative historian Stanisław Estreicher, working briefly as his assistant. While at university, he was president of the Akademickie Koło Kresowe (Academic Club of Those from the Kresy) and joined the organization Myśl Mocarstwowa (Aspirations to Great Power Status), which sought to recreate the political tradition of the Polish-Lithuanian Commonwealth. He was also hostile to antisemitism. According to Janusz Roszko, "he actively opposed the fascist takeover of higher education and defended his colleagues who had a 'Semitic' appearance against pogroms and the violence organized by student corporations."[5] His defense of Jewish students is also confirmed in

---

3 See Anna Pruszyńska, *Między Bohem a Słuczą* (Wrocław: Zakład Narodowy im. Ossolińskich, 2001).

4 Hen, *Nie boję się bezsennych nocy*, 26.

5 Quoted in Jarosław Kurski, "Pruszyński, Ksawery (1907–1950)—pisarz, reporter, dyplomata PRL," *Gazeta Wyborcza*, April 18, 1998.

his mother's autobiography and by his brother Mieczysław in his memoirs.[6] He even fought a duel with an Endek MP, Aleksander Zwierzyński.

An academic career was not to his taste, so Pruszyński began working, first as a proofreader and then as a reporter, for the long-established Kraków daily *Czas* in which Estreicher wrote frequently.[7] It had once been the organ of the Kraków conservatives who in the 1860s had condemned national uprisings as doomed to failure and advocated a compromise with the Habsburgs. In its offices, Pruszyński also rubbed shoulders with the elderly Michał Bobrzyński, one of the architects of Galician autonomy and a former governor of the province. In 1930, he made his debut as a reporter with a series of articles from Hungary and two years later produced a book *Sarajewo 1914, Shanghaj 1932, Gdańsk 193 . . . ?*[8] which argued that the unsettled situation of Gdańsk/Danzig could spark off the next world war. He then moved to Wilno and began to work with Stanisław Mackiewicz, editor of the conservative daily *Słowo* (The Word). Two years later he moved to Warsaw as the paper's correspondent in the capital. At this time he married Maria Meysztowicz, whom he he had met as a student. A member of a landowning family, her father, Alexander Meysztowicz, was a conservative who had become minister of justice after Piłsudski came to power in the coup of May 1926.

Throughout the 1930s, Pruszyński travelled in Poland and Europe, publishing in, among other journals, *Bunt Młodych* (Rebellion of the Young) and its successor *Polityka*, edited by a group of self-described young conservatives, whom he had come to support. A key figure in the group was Jerzy Giedroyc, who after the Second World War was the founder of the Paris-based emigré journal *Kultura*, which was a major contributor to the attempts to rethink Polish politics in the country's new situation. Also influential were the Bocheński brothers, Aleksander and Adolf, with whom the Pruszyński brothers were friendly. At this stage, Pruszyński was an enthusiastic supporter of Piłsudski, describing in *Czas* his meeting with the marshal on November 29, 1931 (as he pointed out in his article the anniversary of the 1830 uprising) as part of a youth delegation. They agreed that their shared background in the Kresy made

---

6   See Mieczysław Pruszyński, *Migawki wspomnień* (Warzsawa: Rosner & Wspólnicy, 2002).

7   *Czas* (The Time)—a Polish daily of patriotic and broadly conservative outlook, launched in 1848 when Kraków was part of the Austro-Hungarian Empire, continued being published there until 1934, then from 1935–1939 in Warsaw.

8   Ksawery Pruszyński, *Sarajewo 1914, Shanghaj 1932, Gdańsk 193 . . .* (Warszawa: Dom Książki Polskiej, 1932).

them superior to other Poles. Pruszyński also explained that, as someone from Ukraine, he was there when the marshal "came to Kiev to liberate my country."[9]

In 1933 Pruszyński travelled to Palestine; the resulting book *Palestyna po raz trzeci* (Palestine for the Third Time),[10] published here for the first time in English, made him a popular and respected journalist. In 1936–1937 he spent six months in Spain reporting for the liberal *Wiadomości Literackie* on the Spanish Civil War; in his articles, he attempted to be fair to both sides. He was fascinated by the atmosphere in republican Madrid. As he wrote in October 1936, "Madrid is more revolutionary than Moscow, more fanatical than Mecca, lives a more intense life than New York."[11] Although he was skeptical of the chances of the revolution proving successful, he saw it as the result of the centuries-long oppression of the Spanish peasantry. For a moment, the peasantry was able to experience freedom and dignity. At the same time, he was well aware of the violence which accompanied it, graphically describing the mass executions carried out by the republicans and the lack of reaction they evoked among the public. Indeed, the central theme of his reportage was the contrast between the elevated goals of the revolution and its grim reality. It was criticized by some of his former allies among the young conservatives as naïve and *Czas* broke off relations with him. [12]

Pruszyński now became increasingly disillusioned with the conservative character of Polish political life, dismayed by the growing antisemitism and anti-Ukrainian sentiment in the country during the 1930s. This is reflected in the articles he published in *Podróż po Polsce* (A Journey through Poland)[13] in which he addressed these questions, as well as unemployment and the radicalization of the countryside. He argued that what was needed for the impoverished peasantry in Poland was not land reform, which would barely alleviate its sufferings, but large-scale industrialization as had occurred before the First World War. As he put it, "[t]he Poznań area and Chicago are the only places where a genuine Polish class revolution has taken place, where the

---

9   Ksawery Pruszyński, "W Belwederze," *Czas*, December 3, 1931.

10 Ksawery Pruszyński, *Palestyna po raz trzeci* (Palestine for the third time) (Wilno: Dom Książki Polskiej 1933).

11 Quoted in Piotr Osęka, "Ksawery Pruszyński—legendarny reporter," *Polityka*, June 25, 2010.

12 His articles were published as *W czerwonej Hiszpanii* (In Red Spain) (Warszawa: Rój, 1937), translated into Spanish as *En la España roja* (Barcelona: Alba, 2007). Extracts from it were reproduced in Pete Ayrton, ed., *No Pasaran!: Writings from the Spanish Civil War* (London: Serpent's Tail, 2017).

13 Ksawery Pruszyński, *Podróż po Polsce* (A Journey through Poland) (Warszawa: Rój, 1936).

peasant has achieved equality and is to be found in shops, banks, law offices, and in school and university. . . . "[14]

This view was also reflected in Pruszyński's report "Przytyk i stragan" (Przytyk and the Market Stall) on the June 1936 trial in Radom of those responsible for the anti-Jewish violence in Przytyk in March of that year:

> The "Przytyk war," the pogrom, the affray which took place here, was a conflict between two groups united by poverty, the poorest of the two nations involved. An outside observer would find it hard to explain what these peasants hoped to gain from taking over Jewish Przytyk, what explains the envy [of their impoverished neighbors] which motivates these people living in miserable hovels.[15]

For Pruszyński, in other countries and in Poland in the nineteenth century, the problems of the countryside had been solved by peasants moving to the towns and finding new opportunities there. Jews had also moved up in the social order. This was no longer occurring in Poland: "Here the development of industry is at a standstill and the annual increase in employment opportunities is minimal in relation to the growing number seeking work. . . . There will be no new generation of Kronenbergs or Blochs [nineteenth-century Jewish industrialists]." People from the countryside who would have been employed by such industrialists now found themselves in brutal competition with poor Jews. Hatred was spreading uncontrollably throughout the country.

Pruszyński now felt increasing sympathy for the views of Bobrzyński and the Galician conservatives, about whom he wrote two articles at this time.[16] Above all, he valued the willingness of the adherents of the Kraków school, the Stańczycy, to express their strong opposition to the complacency and self-satisfaction of most Poles in the face of the obvious defects of their society.

These issues and the need to reestablish a democratic system were also aired in the short-lived biweekly *Problemy*, which Pruszyński founded with his brother and Adolf Bocheński. In addition, he prepared a manuscript on

14 Quoted in Osęka, "Ksawery Pruszyński."
15 Ksawery Pruszyński, "Przytyk i stragan," *Wiadomości Literackie*, July 12, 1936, http://retro-press.pl/wiadomosci-literackie/przytyk-stragan/.
16 Ksawery Pruszyński, "Michał Bobrzyński," *Słowo*, no. 187 (1935) and "Zaduszki wielkiego pisma," *Wiadmości Literackie*, no. 50 (1938), both reproduced in Ksawery Ksawery Pruszyński, *Publicystyka*, vol. 1, *1931–1939: Niezadowoleni i entuzjaści*, ed. Gotfryd Ryka and Janusz Roszko (Warszawa: Państwowy Instytut Wydawniczy, 1990).

Volhynia (Wołyń— a region inhabited by both Poles and Ukrainians) which was ready to be printed in 1939 but was unfortunately lost during the war. He and Adolf Bocheński had even developed a quixotic scheme of embarrassing the government by courting imprisonment in its concentration camp at Bereza Kartuska. Pruszyński now decisively broke with the thinking of the Myśl Mocarstwowa group, seeing the hollowness of the pretensions to Great Power status of the Poland of the colonels who had taken power after the death of Piłsudski in May 1935. As he wrote in 1936:

> In the midst of all the hullabaloo and shouting, the deep conviction that we are marching forward, that we are a power, that we are solving the problems of the countryside, that we are strengthening our state, that we are promoting and encouraging its development, we are gradually, inevitably, falling into a pit.[17]

These views were reflected in the cycle of articles he wrote for the large circulation *Ilustrowany Kurier Codzienny* on the breakup of Czechoslovakia, which were in sharp contrast to the government propaganda praising the acquisition of the Zaolzie region as an indication of Poland's Great Power status. Pruszyński's friend Moses Pomeranz remembers his shocked reaction to seeing Polish troops entering Czechoslovakia: "That's the end of Poland."

In 1940. Pruszyński fought in the Battle of Narvik as an ordinary soldier in the Brygada Podhalańska, subsequently bringing his platoon to Marseille. For his actions in the campaign, which he described in his book *Droga wiodła przez Narvik* (The Road Led through Narvik), he was awarded the Krzyż Walecznych (Cross of the Brave). In *Polish Invasion*,[18] he gave an account of the Polish soldiers in Scotland. Already at this stage he had come to the conclusion that the United Kingdom would not "die" for Polish Wilno or Polish Lwów, since, in his words, "the English are at war with Germany, and as regards Russia, they would give much to draw that country into the war on the side of England."[19]

---

17 Quoted in Osęka, "Ksawery Pruszyński."
18 Ksawery Pruszyński, *Polish Invasion*, trans. Peter Jordan (London: Minerva Publishing Co., 1941).
19 Ksawery Pruszyński, "Sprawa o ktorej się nie mówi, a o której powinno się krzyczeć," *Wiadomości Polskie*, no. 5 (1941), in Ksawery Pruszynski, *Publicystyka*, vol. 2, *1940–1948: Powrót do Soplicowa*, ed. Gotfryd Ryka and Janusz Roszko (Warszawa: Państwowy Instytut Wydawniczy, 1990), 100, 104.

When the Nazis invaded the Soviet Union in June 1941, Pruszyński was asked by General Władysław Sikorski, prime minister of the Polish government in London, to accompany him to Moscow to meet Stalin and to visit the camps where a Polish army was being created. He served as press attaché in the Polish Embassy in Kuibyshev, where foreign embassies had been relocated because of the German threat to Moscow, and edited its journal *Polska*. He described his experiences in *Russian Year: The Notebook of an Amateur Diplomat*,[20] which included a stay in a peasant's hut and a state dinner with Stalin at the Kremlin.

In 1942, after a severe attack of typhus, Pruszyński was forced to return to London. He was now convinced that the Polish government should seek an agreement with Stalin. This was partly the result of his disillusionment with the government-in-exile. He had already produced a pamphlet attacking the accounts of the September campaign of 1939 produced by General Mieczysław Norwid-Neugebauer and Colonel Roman Umiastowski in *Księga ponurych niedopowiedzeń: 1000 mil od prawdy* (The Book of Miserable Failures: 1000 Miles from the Truth).[21] He was aware that the world of the past, of the Second Polish Republic, could not be resurrected. As he wrote in the article "Nasze niebezpieczeństwo" (Our Insecurity), there will be no "new First Brigade [the anti-Russian military formation created by Józef Piłsudski], nor a new Second Brigade . . . . these lines of division are gone forever."[22]

In his article "Puścizna czasów saskich" (The Legacy of Saxon Times), Pruszyński expressed his bitterness at the intrigues and atmosphere within the emigration, the "little London ghetto."[23] His words were harsh:

> In Poland, as we know, it is not wars which are well organized but calumnies. . . . Poland has paid a heavy price for regarding independent thought and freedom of speech as luxuries. There are some luxuries that Poland cannot afford. Poland cannot afford the luxury of national megalomania. Poland cannot afford the luxury of cheap patriotism [*tromtadracja*], the luxury of burning incense, the luxury

---

20 Ksawery Pruszyński, *Russian Year: The Notebook of an Amateur Diplomat* (New York: Roy Publishers, 1944).

21 Ksawery Pruszyński *Księga ponurych niedopowiedzeń: 1000 mil od prawdy* (London: M. I. Kolin, 1941).

22 Hen, *Nie boję się bezsennych nocy*, 22.

23 Ksawery Pruszyński, "Wobec Rosji," *Wiadomości*, October 4, 1942, http://retropress.pl/wiadomosci-polskie/wobec-rosji/.

of bootlicking . . . and, above all, Poland cannot afford the luxury of not thinking.[24]

His disillusionment also extended to interwar Poland. He now observed that in that state, there had been no place for his birthplace because it lay "beyond the Zbrucz." He went on: "Sometimes, when I think of the pacifications of the Tarnopol region, of Bereza and Łuck, of the Orthodox Churches blown up in 1938, of Hrynki and many, many other matters, I think that it was better that there was no such place. . . . "[25]

Pruszyński's decision to call for an understanding with the Soviet Union meant breaking with his former anti-Soviet views. In the pamphlet *Wola władzy* (The Will to Power, 1936), he had justified the Polish involvement in the conflict with the Soviets in 1920:

> We see our struggle at Radzymin [a battle that took place between August 13 and 16, 1920 and was one of the main Polish victories in the 1920 war] as both just and natural. In the eyes of the West, it is often a justification for calling Poland the gendarme of Europe, the hireling of capitalism, the lackey of foreign powers.[26]

In Paris in 1940, in his article "Wilno and Lwów," he had defended the 1921 frontiers of Poland: "These territories constitute nearly half our territory, their inhabitants constitute half the population of our state. We are linked by centuries, not by force . . . [Wilno and Lwów] are like Edinburgh to the British or green Alsace to the French."[27] In May 1941, in "Ultra-red rays," he had compared the Stalinist attempts to Sovietize Poland to those undertaken by the Empress Catherine" "Instead of having to submit to the rod of absolute monarchy, it is submission to the rod of the proletarian dictatorship."[28]

Pruszyński now called for an agreement with Russia which "will always be our nieghbour."[29] "Poland cannot fight on two fronts . . . the fate of Poland will be decided in the pine woods of Karelia and the dusty roads around Smolensk,

---

24 Ibid., 30, 31.
25 Ibid., 24.
26 Ibid., 28.
27 Quoted in Kurski, 'Pruszyński, Ksawery (1907–1950)."
28 Quoted in ibid.
29 Ksawery Pruszyński, "Wrażenia rosyjskie," *Wiadomości Polskie*, no. 1 (1942) quoted in Pruszyński, *Publicystyka*, vol. 2, 171.

Orsza, and Mozhaysk."[30] He set out his new point of view in a polemical article "Wobec Rosji" (Dealing with Russia), published in *Wiadomości*, which had been reestablished in London on October 4, 1942:

> From the beginning of this war, the majority of the Polish nation—and at present the overwhelming majority—is suffering not at the hands of Russia but of Germany and is suffering ever more bitterly, ever more painfully. Germany is the occupier. Germany is the enemy.[31]

The Russians had also suffered terribly at the hands of the Germans and this would provide the basis for a Polish-Russian understanding.

Now praising Roman Dmowski, the former leader of the right-wing National Democrats who had died in January 1939, someone he had long harshly criticized for his understanding of the need for the Poles to compromise with Russia, whatever its political system, Pruszyński argued that the Polish eastern territories would have to be renounced in return for access to the Baltic and Wrocław. Already while in Kuibyshev, he had encountered Polish communists whom he knew from Wilno and had told one of them, Jerzy Putrament, "If you agree to give up Wilno and Lwów, at least demand Wrocław and Szczecin."[32] He was now convinced that the West would not support the Polish cause. In his story written in 1945 "The Shadow of Georgia," Pruszyński describes the fate of a fictional exiled prime minister of that country. When asked why he had given up the political struggle, he told his interlocutor (Pruszyński), "I gave up because I stopped believing. . . . I didn't only believe in Georgia, I believed in the West."[33]

Pruszyński knew these views would be anathema to those who had been deported or imprisoned by the Soviets. He sought justification for them in his own actions: fighting, as a tanker, in General Stanisław Maczek's 1st Armored Division in the battle at Falaise on August 1944, in which he was seriously wounded; and, as a writer, publishing a pamphlet using the historical example of Count Alexander Wielopolski to support his position.[34] He clearly identified strongly with the margrave, who had stressed the need in the 1860s to compromise with Russia and avoid an insurrection. Only partly in jest, Pruszyński signed his name as "Ksawery Wielopolski" in one of his letters to his friend the

---

30 Ksawery Pruszyński, *Margrabia Wielopolski*, 2nd ed. (Warszawa: Pax, 1957), 26–27.
31 Pruszyński, "Wobec Rosji."
32 Quoted in ibid.
33 Quoted in ibid.
34 Pruszyński, *Margrabia Wielopolski*.

journalist Stefania Kossowska during the battle of Falaise.[35] There was a family history here, since the grandfather of his mother Anna had been a strong opponent of the 1830 and 1863 uprisings. According to Anna's memoir:

> My grandfather Mieczysław was a strong opponent of the national uprisings of 1830 and 1863 and of Konarski's conspiracy [an attempt to foment an insurrection in Galicia in 1839], which facilitated the Russification of Volhynia and of the Kresy as a whole from the Dvina to the Dniepr. He was a supporter of the accommodationist policies of Wielopolski. He often said, "If they make a revolution in the Kingdom of Poland, the Polish peasant will survive, but what will remain here?—only the Ruthenian peasant." . . . [A]s a result he would not allow his sons to go "to the forest."[36]

In Pruszyński's view, his critics had underestimated the ability of the Soviets to defeat Hitler. In addition, the war had changed the Soviet Union, which in the future would, he hoped, be ruled by the officers of the Red Army. He had been struck by their "intelligence, independence of thought and solid understanding of the situation." They were marked by their "social conscience, praiseworthy restraint in their manners and modesty."[37] It would be possible for Poland to live in good neighborly relations with a Russia ruled by such men.

Pruszyński was well aware that the policy of giving up areas east of the Bug for territorial acquisitions in the West would be unpopular among Poles. To carry it through, one required a strong individual: "One needs a Chrobry, a Peter the Great, a Kemal Pasha, who can take on his shoulders decisions for the whole nation and for centuries; it is necessary to cut and break."[38]

His disillusionment culminated in his throwing in his lot with the communist-dominated government of Poland, partly as a result of the persuasion of Jerzy Borejsza and Oskar Lange, key figures in that government. In taking this decision, Pruszyński was motivated by his patriotism and belief that he could contribute to the rebuilding of his country; he had no sympathy for communism. He returned to Warsaw in September 1945 on one of the first flights from London to Warsaw and was appointed in November of that year as councilor in the Polish embassy in Washington and then as representative of Polish People's

---

35 Quoted in Kurski, "Pruszyński, Ksawery (1907–1950)."
36 Anna Pruszyńska, *Między Bohem a Słuczą*, 49.
37 Pruszyński, "Wobec Rosji," 231–232.
38 Ibid, 235.

Republic at the newly formed United Nations. In 1947, he headed one of the subcommittees of the UN Special Committee on Palestine; when the resulting UNSCOP proposal was put to the vote as Resolution 181, calling for the partition of Palestine, Pruszyński made a historic speech in its support. At this stage, he seemed to be finding a place in People's Poland. His works were reprinted in large editions and he also now ventured into fiction, publishing two impressive collections of short stories *Trzynaście opowieści* (Thirteen Stories, 1946) and *Karabela z Meschedu* (The Sabre from Meschedu, 1948).

The euphoria did not last. In 1948, Pruszyński was appointed Polish ambassador to the Netherlands. His posting there was certainly a demotion—the Soviets seem to have disapproved of his strongly pro-Israel stance at the UN. Czesław Miłosz described Pruszyński's move to the Hague as "placing him on a sidetrack."[39] Pruszyński himself wrote to his friend Antoni Słonimski in a parody of a letter written to the tsar by a nineteenth century Russian diplomat posted to the Hague: "This town is the most boring in the world. Please, Your Highness, send caviar, vodka, and three horses."[40]

Pruszyński's situation was becoming increasingly difficult as Poland became more and more Stalinist with the intensification of the Cold War. He would probably soon have lost his position and might even have been threatened with a political trial. Certainly he had been told by Jerzy Borejsza that the security services were trying to make a case against him on the grounds that he had been working for Polish intelligence in Madrid in 1936.

He decided to return to Warsaw and was killed on June 13, 1950 in a car accident in Rhynern, south of Hamm, about fifty miles northeast of Düsseldorf. Some have claimed this was not an accident, but was a murder organized either by those in the emigration who resented what they saw as Pruszyński's betrayal or by Stalinists in the Polish government who did not regard him as trustworthy. However, he was well known to be a poor driver and was clearly preoccupied with his situation—it was probably an accident. What made this event even more tragic was that he was returning to Warsaw for his wedding with the twenty-seven-year-old poet Julia Hartwig, with whom he had been involved since 1948 when they had met in the Polish embassy in Paris and with whom he had travelled through France and the Netherlands.

---

39 Quoted in Anna Legeżyńska, "Julia Hartwig. Wdzięczność," *O.pl*, July 24, 2017, http://magazyn.o.pl/2017/anna-legezynska-julia-hartwig-wdziecznosc/#/.

40 Quoted in Kurski, 'Pruszyński, Ksawery (1907–1950).'

Józef Hen observed of Pruszyński's death: "In June 1950, on a German road, there died an outstanding writer, only at the beginning of his creativity. Alongside the death a year later of Borowski (whom he admired) the departure of Pruszyński was the most painful blow to our postwar culture."[41] Antoni Słonimski, the poet and literary critic, who knew Pruszyński well, summed him up as follows: "He was the star of Polish prose, or perhaps its comet who shone brightly but whose path it was difficult to predict. We do not know what its final orbit would have been when it fell to the earth with the heat of youth still unextinguished."[42] Pruszyński was clearly one of the the creators of the Polish school of reportage and his work was highly praised by Ryszard Kapuscíński, a leading member of that school. It is our hope that the publication of his perceptive and prophetic account of the Jewish settlement in Palestine and of the incipient Arab-Jewish conflict will make him better known in the English-speaking world.

—Antony Polonsky

---

41 Hen, *Nie boję się bezsennych nocy*, 32.

42 See "Biografie niezwykłe: Ksawery Pruszyński," Polskie Radio, last modified December 4, 2007, https://www.polskieradio.pl/8/195/Artykul/173742,Biografie-niezwykle-Ksawery-Pruszynski, accessed March 29, 2020.

Selected Bibliography of the Works of Ksawery Pruszyński

Works in English

Adam Mickiewicz: The Life Story of the Greatest Polish Poet. London: Fore Publications, 1950.

No Pasaran! Writings from the Spanish Civil War. Translated by Wiesiek Powaga. London: Serpent's Tail, 2016.

Poland Fights Back. Translated by Peter Jordan. London: Hodder and Stoughton, 1941.

Polish Invasion. Translated by Peter Jordan. London: Minerva Publishing Co., 1941; 2nd ed., Edinburgh: Birlinn, 2010.

Russian Year: The Notebook of an Amateur Diplomat. New York: Roy Publishers, 1944.

Works in Spanish

En la España roja. Translated by Katarzyna Olszewska Sonnenberg, Sergio Trigán, Alba Editorial, 2007.

Works in Polish

Droga wiodła przez Narvik. London: M. I. Kolin, 1941.

Karabela z Meschedu. Opowiadania. Warsaw: Czytelnik, 1948; reprinted, Warsaw: Państwowy Instytut Wydawniczy, 1957.

Księga ponurych niedopowiedzeń: 1000 mil od prawdy. London: M. I. Kolin, 1941.

Margrabia Wielopolski. London: Nakładem "Nowej Polski," 1944; reprinted, Warsaw: Pax, 1957.

Nasi nad Tamizą. Kraków: Wydawnictwo Literackie, 1969.

Opowieść o Mickiewiczu. Warsaw: Państwowy Instytut Wydawniczy, 1956.

Palestyna po raz trzeci. Wilno: Dom Książki Polskiej, 1933.

Podróż po Polsce. Warsaw: Rój, 1937.

Publicystyka. Vol. 1, *1931–1939: Niezadowoleni i entuzjaści.* Edited by Gotfryd Ryka and Janusz Roszko. Warsaw: Państwowy Instytut Wydawniczy, 1990.

Publicystyka. Vol. 2, *1940–1948: Powrót do Soplicowa*. Edited by Gotfryd Ryka and Janusz Roszko. Warsaw: Państwowy Instytut Wydawniczy, 1990.

Sarajewo 1914, Szanghaj 1932, Gdańsk 193 . . . ? Warsaw: Dom Książki Polskiej, 1932.

Trzynaście opowieści. Warsaw: Czytelnik, 1946.

W czerwonej Hiszpanii. Warsaw: Rój, 1937.

Walczymy. Jerusalem: W Drodze, 1943.

Wybór pism 1940–1945. Introduction by Włodziemierz Odejewski. Warsaw: Oficyna Wydawnicza Rytm, 1989.

Wybór pism publicystycznych. 2 vols. Kraków: Wydawnictwo Literackie, 1966.

Introduction

Ksawery Pruszyński (December 4, 1907– June 13, 1950) was one of the leading Polish journalists in the first half of the twentieth century. According to Ryszard Kapuściński, it was thanks to him that reportage became not only a product of the eye, but also of the mind. Pruszyński was born into a Polish aristocratic family in what is now Ukraine, but the Bolshevik Revolution forced the family out of their estates and, rather impoverished, they settled in the newly independent Poland. His widowed single mother, in spite of financial difficulties managed to send both Ksawery and his brother Mieczysław to the Jagiellonian University, where they studied law.

It was there, while active in a conservative student organization called Myśl Mocarstwowa (Aspirations to Great Power Status)[1] that they met Mojżesz Pomeranz. Formed in the 1920s, Aspirations to Great Power Status (AGPS) was a political movement active in academic centers across Poland with a largely upper- and middle-class membership. Akin to today's think tanks, it engaged in outlining a political agenda for the new Polish state to be developed and implemented by its young elites. While its main goal was to build a strong modern state, at the same time it idealized the old Jagiellonian Polish-Lithuanian Union which functioned as a multiethnic and multinational commonwealth. Unlike its rival National Democracy (ND), which wanted to fuse the ethnic and the national as the core of Polish identity and the foundation of the state, AGPS's leading thinkers (such as Rowmund Piłsudski and Jerzy Giedroyc)[2] proposed an inclusive civil platform representing all ethnic strands

---

1   Aspirations to Great Power Status Group—this translation of Myśl Mocarstwowa tries to capture the leading thought at the foundation of the group, namely Marshal Piłsudski's warning: "Poland will be a Great Power or she will not exist." Piłsudski thought it was only then that Poland would be able to resist the relentless imperialist pressures from Russia and Germany.

2   Jerzy Giedroyc (1906–2000)—Polish journalist, political activist, and legendary editor of the highly influential political and literary magazine *Kultura* (1947–2000), which was pub-

within the structure of state. At the international level, it aimed at a modern kind of commonwealth, a federalist structure comprising former nations of the pre-Partitioned Poland, such as Lithuania and Ukraine, as well as those of the Russian Empire, such as Georgia. This new formation of a string of independent states was supposed to create a secure buffer for Poland stuck between Russia and Germany.

The standard-bearing periodical in which AGPS debated ideas was the tellingly titled *Bunt Młodych* (Rebellion of the Young), run by Jerzy Giedroyc. As well as Giedroyc and Pruszynski, the periodical's other leading authors were Ksawery's brother Mieczysław and the Bocheński brothers Józef Maria, Aleksander, and Adolf. Seen from today's perspective, the extent to which Pruzyńsky and Giedroyc shared their political roots and direction of evolution is remarkable.

National Democracy's antisemitism was one of the key reasons Ksawery joined AGPS; and it was a street fight with ND activists, in which he was wounded, that cemented his friendship with Mojżesz Pomeranz. It was later—and with the help of Pomeranz, who organized support from his Jewish colleagues—that Pruszyński successfully campaigned for the position of chair of the University's Association of Law Students, which was planning to remove Jewish students from its organization. This victory was especially satisfying as only a few months before Hitler had come to power in Germany. Ousting the ND leadership significantly limited their previously undisputed influence within the university.

Ksawery's and Mojżesz's friendship continued outside the lecture halls, when Ksawery and (his brother) Mieczysław often visited the Pomeranz family and, beyond graduation, when Ksawery got a job at Cracow's *Czas*, where he went from proofreading to reporting to writing his first book—*Sarajewo 1914, Shanghaj 1932, Gdańsk 193 . . . ?* An early example of Pruszyński's prophetic gift, the book warned of the possible outbreak of another world war.

At the same time, Mojżesz opened his own legal practice and became increasingly interested in the Zionist idea of establishing and building a new state for the Jews.

By the early 1930s, Zionism had emerged as one of the main topics of political debate among Jews, as well as non-Jews, and naturally between Mojżesz

---

lished in Maison-Lafitte near Paris; from 1930, he was the editor of *Bunt Młodych* (later *Polityka*). Throughout his life, he supported the rights of Polish ethnic minorities and friendly cooperation between Central European nations, a political program based on Józef Piłsudski's Prometheist project. After the Second World War, he argued for the peaceful acceptance of Poland's new borders, but nevertheless decided to remain in exile. (Transl.)

and Ksawery. Being both deeply committed to the idea of the state as an intellectual and political construct—as distinct from the National Democrats' stress on the primacy of the nation as defined by ethnicity—it didn't take long for Mojżesz to persuade Ksawery about the value of on-the-ground reportage from the Zionist front lines in Mandate Palestine; they were both interested to see if the dream of returning to Eretz Yisrael had a chance of becoming reality and to find out how the Zionists were going about it.

***

Pruszyński travelled to Palestine in 1932. Initially, he wrote his reports for the Vilnius weekly *Słowo* (The Word), subsequently collecting them in the book *Palestyna po raz trzeci* (Palestine for the Third Time) republished in 1936 by Warsaw's Rój, a publishing house run by another pioneer of Polish reportage Pomeranz.

Palestine was the result of a six-week tour across the *yishuv* (Jewish Palestine), most of it on foot, during which Pruszyński visited all its legendary cities and famous *kibbutzim* and met all kinds of people—from Zionists, communists, and Arabs to disaffected Polish Jews who couldn't wait to get out, or simply couldn't. Pruszyński's growing respect and enthusiasm for the Zionist project is palpable in the text. As a Pole born into a formally nonexistent country, but who had seen it resurrected after 130-odd years of partitions, he was particularly sensitive to the plight of a nation in need of a state; and as an educated, thinking man he was also interested in how the state should function to provide all its citizens with the conditions to thrive economically and culturally in a secure environment.

Based on his experience of his own native country, Pruszyński was very much aware that it would not be an easy task, but the more he explored the more he was impressed by the efforts of the pioneers, old and new, who were trying out new ways of life and new forms of statehood. He was struck by the economic success of the potential state machinery and noticeably moved by individual stories—triumphs and failures, successful (and unsuccessful) escapes from poverty and antisemitism—all of them lives devoted to making the dream come true. And being brought up steeped in history in an old Polish tradition and at the same time in a new multiethnic Polish state, he was also very much aware of the dangers of nationalism. In the case of Mandate Palestine, he understood the emerging conflict between, on the one hand, awakening Arab ethnic and national identity and, on the other, the Zionist project—both rooted in the idea that ethnic identity equals nation equals state.

The book is unusual not just because Pruszyński, a Polish aristocrat, was totally won over by the idea and saw that creating a modern State of Israel was a firm possibility, but also—and this is classic Pruszyński—in that it turned out to be quite prophetic in foreseeing that the foundations of that state had a built-in fault line. In conversation, he and an Arab nationalist consider that the political complexities of the Mandate and the balance of power in the Middle East could be "corrected" by another major war, just as the Great War altered the situation by demoting Turkey from its position as the major regional power. He also sensed that the fermenting Arab-Jewish conflict was going to be a time bomb, which no one would know how to defuse.

This was Pruszyński's first truly successful book and, if it did not make him quite the household name he became later, it certainly advanced him into the first rank of journalists in prewar Poland. It had a big, if mixed, reception: ambivalent and confused in the Polish press; curious, even enthusiastic, in Jewish forums of all political shades. Following his return from Palestine and the publication of the book, the author embarked on a number of tours, mostly to the eastern borderlands, from Vilnius, through Lublin, to Lviv, drawing fascinated audiences everywhere, mostly Jewish, of course, but not exclusively. The popularity of the book among Jewish readers is attested to by a number of reviews, such as Heszel Klepfisz's[3] "Pruszyński na Szczęśliwej Wyspie" (Pruszyński on the Island of Happiness) published in his collected essays *Przedwojenny świat przez pryzmat młodego Żyda polskiego* (The Prewar World through the Eyes of a Young Polish Jew [Tel Aviv: Eran Reut, 1999]).

***

Palestine for the Third Time was not the last word Pruszyński had on the Zionist project or Polish Jewish relations, writing articles like "Przytyk i stragan" (Przytyk and a Market Stand), about a pogrom carried out in a small town near Radom in 1936, and short stories such as "Karabela z Meschedu" (A Sabre from Mashhad, 1948), about a Jew who joined the Polish II Corps to fight Hitler. But in summer 1936, Pruszyński's attention was captured by the Spanish Civil War and in the autumn he set off for his next journalistic assignment, which resulted in another masterpiece of reportage *Inside Red Spain*.

---

3   Heszel Klepfisz (1910–2004)—Polish-Israeli journalist, philosopher, and historian; during World War II, he was an officer and rabbi in the Polish Army; after the war, he lived in Costa Rica and Panama. He was the author of *End of an Era: Eastern European Jewry Roots and Uniqueness* [Yiddish], 5 vols. (Jerusalem: n.p., 1989); he also wrote in Hebrew and Polish. (Transl.)

That might have been the natural end of his Palestinian adventure and pre-occupation with that Zionist project. Then came the war and the Shoah and, in one of those fine twists of fate, Pruszyński found himself again involved in the Zionist project, and this time not only as an observer but quite instrumentally too.

In 1947, while in New York working as an advisor to the Polish mission at the UN, he was invited by the ambassador of the new communist Polish Republic to the US, Oskar Lange, to join the Ad Hoc Committee for the Palestinian Question, a newly formed part of the UN Special Committee on Palestine (UNSCOP). It was on the strength of *Palestine for the Third Time* that he was considered an expert on the question. It was also his experience as a diplomat during the war, when posted in Soviet Union and working with General Sikorski who was negotiating with Stalin, that made him uniquely qualified for the job. By then, Pruszynski's political position had evolved from the idealistic conservatism of the Aspirations to Great Power Status group of the 1920s through an increasingly critical and openly hostile attitude towards the post-Piłsudski colonel's regime, to pragmatic center-left statism. Following his experience of the Spanish Civil War and the deep disappointment of Yalta's realpolitik,[4] he decided to work alongside Poland's new communist regime— for the good of the (next) new state.

Pruszyński was elected as head of one of the subcommittees— Subcommittee One tasked with preparing the legal groundwork and drawing up the geographical borders for a new state to be proposed following British withdrawal from the Mandate Palestine. He committed wholeheartedly to the work, believing that the Jews deserved a state of their own, while fully aware that the festering Arab-Jewish conflict required some kind of guarantee for the rights of the Palestinians; the final recommendation of his subcommittee was two separate states—one Arab, the other Jewish. He worked tirelessly in support of this plan; according to historical records, he had great negotiating skills, dealing with pressure applied from different, often directly opposed, directions, and always with the clear aim of bringing about the creation of a Jewish state. This is best illustrated by the two speeches he delivered as chairman of Subcommittee One: the first was at the final, closing session of the Ad Hoc Committee, where he explained in detail the complexities of the proposal

---

4   At the Yalta conference, Roosevelt, Churchill, and Stalin divided their spheres of influence, turning Poland into a Soviet satellite state, which made many of Pruszynski's friends of a similar political outlook, like Jerzy Giedroyc, decide not to return to communist Poland (Transl).

and why it was still the best possible in the circumstances; the second was on November 29 before General Assembly's vote on Resolution 181, when he passionately argued for the creation of a Jewish state. Legend has it that this speech swung the vote—after all, the proposal was passed with a majority of one. The mechanics of the vote were probably less straightforward, but nevertheless, it has gone down in history as *the* defining moment in the history of the State of Israel, which was founded later in May 1948.

✱✱✱

In November 1947, Mojżesz Pomeranz wrote to Pruszyński:

> I cannot express in this letter the admiration and enthusiasm inspired by each of your speeches. Someone said that if you came to Palestine, people would greet you with flowers, like another Balfour, only with greater love. Anti-Polish sentiments which are undoubtedly present in the Jewish society in Palestine, . . . are fading away today and doubtless it is thanks to Ksawery Pruszyński, who is saving the good name of the Polish nation and enhancing Poland's.[5]

Amidst the ensuing frantic protests of the Arab delegations and the increased pressure of, and arm-twisting from, the Jewish one, Pruszyński was quietly removed from his position by his superiors, somewhat alarmed by his determined support for the Jewish state while Stalin was still weighing his options. Nevertheless, in that final speech on the day of the vote he reiterated his—and what he believed to be Poland's—official position:

> Gentlemen, you are right to claim that in this whole matter Poland has demonstrated more of a concern for the fate of Israel then have other nations. We accept these—presumably sarcastic—words as the highest praise of Polish foreign policy. . . . We have been defending and will always defend every just cause, which is why we have been defending and will defend the Jewish cause. . . . We also defended it for other reasons, namely because no other nation understands like the Polish nation the longing for one's own land, the land that belong

---

5   M. Pruszyński, *Mojżesz i Ksawery* (Warszawa: Wydawnictwo Twój Styl, 1999); from Bożena Szaynok, *Poland-Israel 1944–1968: In the Shadow of the Past and of the Soviet Union*, trans. Dominika Ferens (Warszawa: Wydawnictwo IPN, 2012).

to one's ancestors, where one would not have to suffer the fate of an intruder or pilgrim.[6]

This book provides a fascinating vignette into what the Zionist dream was in the early 1930s and invites us to reflect on what has become of it now.

—Wiesiek Powaga

---

6   K. Pruszyński, "Polska a Erec," quoted from the Polish-Language Zionist periodical *Opinia* [Łódź; Tel-Aviv], no. 28 (1948), in Szaynok, *Poland-Israel 1944–1968*, 402–405c.

Foreword

Iwent to Palestine because I was struck by the difference in tone when Poles talk about the "new Palestine," and when it is discussed increasingly so, increasingly among Jews. I went there as a journalist to investigate reports of a religious phenomenon, which brought to mind the case of Theresa of Konnersreuth.[1] It had not yet been decided whether what was involved in was a miracle or a fraud.

If this book has any value for Poles it is to make them consider the consequences of a development whose significance has not yet been fully recognized—conserving traditions of the ghetto, on the one hand, and of assimilation, on the other, displaced by that of the rebuilding of Zion. If this book has any value for Jews familiar with the Palestine project, it is as the opinion of an outsider, a neutral witness watching from the sidelines.

The fact that three million Jews live in Poland today provides justification for my addressing this issue. Whether we like it or not, we cannot remain indifferent to their aspirations, nor can they ignore what we think about them. Poland seems to be a highly suitable vantage point from which to observe the efforts of this new country, which now, before our eyes, is entering history, and not for the first time.

---

1   Theresa Neumann of Konnersreuth—German mystic and stigmatic, who claimed a number of miraculous cures and abilities, which after tests were proved false. (Transl.)

1

On a Bunk Bed with the
Halutzim

The *Dacia* is a small old-fashioned steamship plying from Constança to Haifa. On the whole, this is a less frequented route; excellent modern Italian ships sailing from Trieste to Jaffa have taken over most of the traffic. The *Dacia* has been left with two principal groups of passengers: tourists attracted by the picturesque passage around Constantinople and the Golden Horn and poor Jewish immigrants. This was clear on my first evening. The *Dacia* has four classes of accommodation, but in fact there are only two—the tourist class and the *halutz* class.

On the lowest deck, four meters below the waterline, there is a long wooden warren, called "fourth class." Along its walls are placed two-tier, low wooden bunks. On the better bunks, one can sit without knocking one's head on the boards of the upper. There are officially about fifty places. But fourth class has no admission limits. A hundred, two hundred—it's the captain's privilege. In this case, there are eighty-seven. The figure fluctuates from port to port, now higher, now lower. But all the way throughout the journey there will be those who won't have any choice but to sleep on top of their own goods and chattels piled in the middle of the space allocated to fourth class. Some try to escape to the half-deck: at night the smell is more bearable, but the heat from the engines still makes it a difficult berth. But it is slightly more comfortable than the actual fourth-class accommodation.

The great lounge of the ship was lavishly illuminated even before the anchor was raised. It was host to the highlife of the upper class, which had just emerged from the dining rooms below the deck. Frocks. Cards. Music. Through the round window with a view of the deck one could see ice-creams melting in silver chalices sitting on mounds of ice cubes, also melting though not as fast. The upper-deck classes haven't blended yet, each party is separate, in its own glory and distinction, just like King Carol II in his admiral's uniform in the huge painting on the main wall. Gentlemen embellished with medals walk around or stand. They are showing off. Massive club chairs and small plush seats are empty. Three floors down, there is not one suitcase free. Just a moment ago, as the ship was leaving the harbor, everyone sang the anthem of the *halutzim*, which slightly alarmed the captain's young assistant—it could have been something communist and could have provoked the police. Now they all laugh loudly, talk, and shout across the room. They are all young.

I am the only non-Jew among the eighty-seven. With only a few exceptions, they are all young Romanian Jews. On their way to Palestine. Hence the joy. They are going for good. That is to say, officially only two-thirds of all immigrants have a proper certificate entitling them to stay permanently, but the others also don't intend to return. They were brought up and schooled by the Jewish youth organizations, which transformed them into settlers and workers, *halutzim. Halutz*, a Hebrew word, means "pioneer." And these are young *halutzim*, the pioneers in an endeavor, which, even now, many speak as of as utopian and a chimera, yet which has already produced results far greater than those dreamt of by its father founders. Few are more than twenty-one. Most are eighteen to twenty. Girls too. But there are fewer of them than boys. And they are quieter and perhaps not as joyful.

The only boundaries that persist—or, rather, which have been formed by the living conditions in fourth class—are those of the bunks. The need to share imposes closeness. The bunks are like wards, town districts. The three or four people who happen to occupy one make up an instant *hevra*, and a well-bonded one at that; so much so that, even if the only common language is Russian (many of the passengers hail from Bessarabia), they are all, from the word go, on first-name terms, just because they have dropped their baggage here rather than there. Of course they have not known each other for long. Quite the opposite. But, it is they, the *hevra*, who will make sure no one "borrows" the mirror left on your pillow when you nip off onto the deck; the *hevra* won't let your next bunk neighbor move your luggage. But also—the *hevra* will look at you askance if you share your Constança oranges, or even a cupful of tea from your thermos flask, with another bunk in preference to your own. Varied and strange, fleeting and widely differing from each other are the instantly acquired habits of the bunk bed *hevras*.

Then comes the night: the stormy and heavy-as-lead Black Sea night. Then come the seven days and nights, a whole week spent on the same deck, in the same bunk. Only in barracks, prison, or immigrants' tents does one breathe the same air that had been exhaled by a hundred other lungs, and only there does one live one's life so intimately interwoven with everything else done in other lives. The tighter the weave and the bigger the crush of the *Dacia*'s fourth class, the closer, friendlier, and more brotherly are your ties with the accidentally met Jewish toiler from Chişinău or Botoşani. The black Hebrew letters on their "certificates" granting them leave to settle in Palestine will remain for a long time, perhaps forever, a hieroglyphic to a non-Jew. But sharing a bunk opens up to him an unknown world behind seven mountains and seven seas—their inner world. Seven days on the lowest deck of the immigrants' boat can have a profound effect. Life down below possesses a great fusing power.

***

Moses Schamroth is one of those with whom I fused most quickly. He is twenty, looks physically a bit of a weakling. For the last ten years he has lived in Bucharest, working for a Jewish daily newspaper. He is intelligent, his reading list lifting him way above the standard of regular education he has completed, which ended somewhere around the third year of secondary school. Indeed, the whole of the *Dacia*'s fourth class contains barely four *halutzim* with any university education and none of them graduated. Moses Schamroth likes to share his knowledge. He does it conscientiously and methodically.

"What make you, the young ones, want to emigrate to Palestine?"

"Look," says Moses, "there are four different motives, some stronger, some weaker. First—national tradition. It's our fatherland. It's a motive shared by everyone, but almost never as the main, decisive one. Except perhaps for the Zionist-revisionists, the reactionaries. But there are none of them here. . . . "

"What else?"

"Secondly," says the *halutz*, "the crisis. For a young Jew who doesn't have money, getting any sort of employment is becoming increasingly difficult, even hopeless. These people no longer can live in a foreign society, they can't make even five lei a day. Palestine provides an opportunity for work which at least offers sustenance. It's a non-ideological motive. If it's the only motive someone has for emigration—well, he won't last long. Then there is this motive, at the moment very strong, perhaps the strongest—I don't know if others have told you, but we all are going to join agricultural collectives, the communes. At the moment, the Palestinian and Russian collectives are the only places where the world is developing new ways of life, where it has freed itself of the dominance of the nonproducing classes. It is our ambition to take part in this liberation movement, in this great endeavor. Our Palestine will show the world the way."

Schamroth becomes enthusiastic, giving short firm answers to my quickly thrown questions. I tell him that Zionism is not a red movement.

"Yes," he agrees, "but we are red. . . . "

"National communists, then?"

He laughs—"Yes, you could say that. I was a communist," he says. "When they convinced me that communism could be linked with the national idea, I became a Zionist."

But Moses Schamroth became a Zionist also for another reason—he does not believe communism will become a reality any time soon. "Communism has come into this world too early. It was a premature, war-induced birth. That's why it was so bloody; it's lame." (Moses Schamroth is too sober to be led astray by the prospect of five-year plans, and too honest to lie; he doesn't hide the failures of communism, he seeks to explain them.) Communism, in his opinion, turns people off for two reasons: the scale of sacrifice in human life it has cost to introduce it and its coercive character, all the way from A to B. And lo and behold, in Palestine they have built the foundations of communism without bloodshed or coercion in a manner that is acceptable to people, and will lead them out of the crisis. The great historical mission of Israel.

Apart from the Soviet or Palestine communes, there is one other such collective in this world, the one formed by the young *halutzim* of the ship. The views of Moses Schamroth, whose influence is not limited to his bunk friends, are shared, in various shades of intensity, by all of them. But Moses Schamroth, a self-educated orphan, has missed one motive, which perhaps counts as emotional but is very strong among the *halutzim*—freedom.

***

Its strength among these young half-communists was revealed to me by Klara Zalatkowska. Unlike the sickly weakling Moses Schamroth, she is a strong, handsome girl, almost beautiful and doesn't look Jewish. She is the daughter of a "pure proletarian family"—as stressed a couple of times by Moses Schamroth, who alas (as he says himself) lacks such a pure proletarian origin. Her education is rather basic and rests, it seems, chiefly on sitting through a number of discussions conducted by others. Still, among the *Dacia* girls she is the most intelligent.

"Practically everyone in the country"—here "the country" means "Romania"—"leads a very sad life. Not just hard, as in difficult living conditions, but sad. It's unbelievable how fierce everyday quarrels between young and old in the same family can be. Our old folks have changed very little—they are just like they were twenty, thirty years ago. When I look at the Romanian girls, I have a feeling they are not as modern as us Jewish girls. And yet their parents have kept up with the times better than ours. A good relationship with parents begins when we leave home. The further away the better."

This gap between generations seems to be a profound problem in a poor Jewish society. "And"—Klara continues—"young people these days feel completely different, different from their parents and from . . . all other things. . . . "

"From the whole world?" I try to lend her a spark when she loses hers and can't find the word.

"Yes," she lights up again, "the whole world. You see, somehow, things happened the way they are. Romanian newspapers write that young Jews are all communists. Well, I've seen all sorts, and I see it differently. They are not communists, even if they sign up for communism. They only go against what there is and try out communism; maybe they'll find what they are looking for. They are trying Zionism too. Now they are looking here, but tomorrow somewhere else."

This conversation took place on the fourth day of our journey. We stood on the top deck by the lifeboats, watching the Piraeus lighthouse turning its light on and off every thirty seconds.

"And why are they moving on to Zionism?"

"Look, this may be the easiest thing to explain in all this confusion. They don't want to wait. They want to create for themselves the kind of life they want—for themselves. So they take the first opportunity. Agricultural collectives in Palestine? It's like we've already jumped over the whole revolution and landed in the new system. It's quicker. Indeed—it's already there."

Two days later Klara returned to our conversation.

"It's not just the possibility of an immediate start in living one's own dreams life and fulfilling one's social needs that draws people to Palestine. Another thing is at play too—the young, even those fully converted to communism, can't be sure that once they start their lives they won't be bitterly disappointed. And then it may be hard to 'turn the world around' again. That's one thing. The other—'the Russian thing,' it's already hardened and solidified, and it's become what it is. . . . "

"It's become an icon," I joke. But Klara doesn't catch my meaning. I suggest the stiff, frozen gestures of figures in Byzantine and Russian Orthodox holy paintings.—"Yes, like those icons!" she understands. "*Trogat' vospreshchaetsia.*"[1] But in Palestine everything is just beginning, and follows its own path. Now they are trying this, now something else. There, we will try it all ourselves. If we don't like it, we change it. If I don't like it—I walk away."

"And you, yourself—how are you going to try?"

Klara, like many other girls, doesn't quite know. Of course, a collective to start with; she needs a safety net or at least a place to sleep. Later—"*kak luchshe*," as they say in Russian: follow a better option.

***

That laughing, serious girl is one of a few who are traveling to Palestine on their own. Most of them have friends whom they've often known for years, steady boyfriends, even husbands. In a way, they are all on the run from home. It's only at first glance that they look the poorest of poor. On the neighboring bunk sleeps the son of a wealthy corn merchant from Buzău, though I learned about it from one of our fellow travelers. He himself mentioned it only once in passing. Moses Schamroth pointed at him with disdain. But he is not the only one Moses Schamroth does not like. He also dislikes a small group of girls of delicate build, dressed with a certain—but how modest—pretension to chic.

"They won't be going to work, for sure," he said one day.

"They are not weaker than you," I replied.

I didn't quite understand then how much unintended cruelty there was in my off-the-cuff remark. My comrade turned away and avoided me for the rest of the day. We did return to our long talks, though, and I tried to assure him how work builds up strength, how the southern climate quickly turns one into a man, that he was no wimp. But the shadow of that exchange hung over us. I'd struck the weakling's weakest side.

At just about that time, there took place the following incident. One morning, very early, on the top deck by the helm, I saw a couple of old Jews and three young ones from third class. They'd put on their ritual vestments and were reading a prayer. It was a great scene: Hasidim crossing the Ionian

---

1 Rus.: "Do not touch!" (Transl.)

Sea on their way to Jerusalem. I would have loved to have taken a photo, but feared offending them. Then I saw my friend coming from the bow of the ship. He saw the scene and smiled at me. A long silence fell on the ship and the sea. The old Jews were rocking, an ironic smile of the young Jew: I couldn't take my eyes off them.

Later that day, I started talking with the pioneers about religion. It didn't exist for them. In various different ways. Moses Schamroth once more showed himself to be a historical materialist, a fully-fledged communist, if heretical in terms of nationalism. He disliked religion, mocked ritual. Others had a different approach: whether God existed or not was an obscure and doubtful matter. What was certain, or less doubtful, was that their religious practices (and the practices of other faiths, they added with equal certainty)—was nonsense. It had made sense in the past, perhaps, when religion was an indispensable tool for enforcing certain hygienic and social practices, and instilling a sense of national identity. Today, it is not needed. And anyway—the only important thing today, the only thing tangible—is Palestine.

2

The Dust of the Road

"The Greek land will greet you with sunshine and wine!"—thus spoke a tourist guide. I remembered it as I was gathering all my knowledge about ancient Greece (gymnasium of the traditional type) to choose one "truly Greek" dish from an unbelievably long menu. Only at the last moment did I save myself from the embarrassment of ordering *felenes oites*, which turned out to be a Wiener schnitzel. What bad luck to arrive in Hellas only to find Galicia.[1] I remembered vaguely that in one of the last parts of the *Apology of Socrates* (or was it in *Crito*?—have I forgotten it all?) the wise Plato gave a long list of Attic dishes. Plato was not a plebeian, but a philosopher, so he knew his cuisine. I could not recall anything apart from *daimons*,[2] who sit inside man and advise him—or so claimed Socrates before the judges—what not to do, but not, alas, what to do. The Wiener schnitzel was the last thing about which I let the waiter advise me; I decided to take pot luck. And so, instead of soup I ended up with a rather odd salad of mushrooms and olives, which had to be rapidly followed by a small glass of Attic spirits, no chaser.

All I had tried so far was rather dubious. I kept looking and looking until I found this: *ba-bu-nia*[3]—I deciphered. It stood out on the page, rendered in beautiful Greek calligraphy, but sounded Polish—a "little grandma." Damn, I thought, whoever thought of giving a dish a name like this. It's not exactly a mouthwatering advertisement. Not to mention the associations of

---

1 Galicia—historical and geographical region between Central and Eastern Europe, following the partitions of Poland 1772–1918, part of the Austro-Hungarian Empire; from 1918–1939, the western part of eastern Poland; after World War II, Western Ukraine. (Transl.)

2 *Daimon; deamon* (Greek)—an inner or attendant spirit or inspiring force. Socrates claimed to have lived his life according to the dictates of his *daimon*. (Transl.)

3 *Babunia*—Pol.: endearing diminutive form of *babcia*—grandmother. (Transl.)

cannibalism: the idea of consuming somebody who might be someone's dear little grandma—no, thanks. If it were wine, that would be a different story: a discreet allusion to its age. But meat! For a moment I sat paralyzed by the thought—a grandma steak. . . . But the waiter managed to dispel my fear by explaining with the help of his hands that *babunia* was a fish. Phew, alright, fish I can do.

Just like in a Parisian restaurant (I hear that's how they do it there), I was presented with a big metal pan with not one, but a whole school of grandmas, frisky in the water as though they were their own grandchildren. Their scales had a pleasant silvery-red hue. I assumed the face of a connoisseur and picked the first that swam to my finger. It was immediately taken away for frying. Which didn't last long, and after a short while I was served that very same grandma on a silver platter, stuffed with something mysterious and covered in yellow-red sauce. Of the sauce, I knew only that it was composed with the sweet wine of Euboea. Or was it Salamis? That made me think of the great Battle of Salamis against the Persians, and I tucked into my grandma. With great gusto and no scruples.

* * *

That afternoon taught me one great truth, still not revealed in a Baedeker. Namely, that a man can get lost not only in an Athenian menu, but also in Athenian streets. I learned this valuable lesson somewhere between the parliament (as pompous as it is banal) and the Acropolis. I was looking for the shortest possible route to the top of the hill rising right in front of me. From the moment I set forth, the "shortest" started getting longer and the "route" turned into a labyrinth. When "possible" began to turn into "impossible," after a walk along the *hodós* of Lycurgus (which *hodós*—road—turned out to be the only one worth getting lost on) I came out onto a wide square. And here: noise, police, a demonstration. The demonstration itself was about thirty-people strong, but demonstrate they did. The police was dispersing them by waving their batons in the air. The demonstrators obligingly split to the left and right. The police, somewhat out of breath, ran hither and thither and regrouped when it became clear that the "masses" were moving onto another square, where another exercise of baton waving had to be performed. What lovely demonstrations they have in Athens.

The good-natured police do not tear communist posters off the wall, so at the nearest kiosk I could read a great proclamation to *ergotetes kai agrotetes* (workers and peasants) to join the "Pan-Athenian Marx Jubilee." It was the beautiful word "pan-Athenian" that caught my eye: a truly Hellenic form. But meanwhile, an asphalted road had unfolded before me, a grove clinging to a rock came into sight, and lo!—the Acropolis.

The act of entry had a mythological flavor for me too, for at the gate I found two of my fellow travelers waiting, but not entering. They had not been admitted, just like those souls who had no obol in their mouths to pay Charon his fee. The Charons of today's Acropolis demand more than the journey to the lea on the other side of the Styx costs: fifty drachma. Still, one hasn't read Homer in the original or carried Demosthenes' *Philippics* in one's travel bag for nothing—I was let through. And then I was struck by the difference between those two stone-dead cities, Constantinople and Athens: so alike, and yet so different.

Constantinople is a city in mourning. From the street shoeshine man setting up his brass receptacles in all shapes and sizes at the gate of any mosque with good tourist traffic, to the old mufti proceeding with the dignity of a great lord—everyone is in mourning for the good old days. Hagia Sofia, Sultan Ahmed, and Sultan Bayezid are in mourning. But Athens is not.

Athens, too, has one Great Dead. Exhumed after many years with pious care, his tomb was searched with equally pious diligence for any spiritual remains. But the Great Athenian Dead has been dead for a long time. The mourning period is over. And there is no sign of mourning anywhere, not a shade of grief.

The Acropolis, apart from the ruins of three temples, is only a field covered with stones. They lie next to each other like broken pieces of a something which no power will ever restore to wholeness. Taking in the sight from under the heavy columns of the Temple of Theseus, it looks like a cemetery.[4] And it is.

In the setting sun, the Dorian columns of the Acropolis glow not just with the whiteness of the marble, but also with the yellow stains of damage inflicted by rain and air. They seem to be utterly drained of color, like a human skull buried for centuries in the ground. The earthy gray walls of Constantinople sometimes look like a corpse that has not been removed from a catafalque.

---

4   Temple of Theseus (or Theseion)—according to legend, the temple housed the remains of the Greek hero Theseus; the name was still in use during the author's visit, but later archeological research confirmed it was in fact dedicated to Hephaestus. (Transl.)

3

The Land without Crises

"All countries today have the ambition to close the year's budget without deficit. Palestine's budget for years has closed in surplus.

"Defense takes a huge chunk of all budgets everywhere. Palestine pays only for the upkeep of a few divisions.

"All countries close their borders with high trade tariffs; Palestine, with few exceptions, knows only fiscal tariffs.

"Everywhere capital is investment-bound or there is none; in Palestine it is plentiful and it's liquid.

"Most countries have large, complex tax systems; Palestine knows only the simplest income tax and runs a protective rather than an exploitative policy towards the taxpayer.

"And so, while everywhere else there is unemployment, Palestine has jobs to spare."

Such was the short answer to the question, what explains the current economic boom in Palestine? The answer was given to me by Bernard Hausner, the consul of the Polish Republic in Tel Aviv. We were standing on the balcony of the big building in which the Polish consulate has its offices. Below, Tel Aviv spread before us in a wide swathe of white houses and streets caught between Jaffa Bay and the green belt of orange groves. But what we were looking at now was not the sea or the country, but the city. We were watching it grow.

To the left and to the right, below us and further ahead, even far away—building sites. Montefiore Street was no longer in the suburbs. Everywhere, here and as far as the eye could see—building sites. Fawn patches of sand and white piles of cement, the concrete pillars of future houses, shuttering and foundations all around. It looked as if the dunes were swelling up and giving birth to forms that elsewhere had already hardened and set as the walls of new houses.

The first thing that struck me in Palestine was the country's prosperity. After gray, impoverished Turkey, and Greece trying to hide its poverty, the country simply radiated with prosperity. There is no crisis here. In Haifa, a great port of the future, a bricklayer earns ten to fifteen zlotys a day. The bricklayers here are mostly uncertified; among the *halutzim* there are very few people who haven't yet worked, even if only for a stint, as bricklayers. It is quite symbolic that at one time or another two-thirds of last eight years' immigrants have worked as bricklayers. The cost of living has been estimated at five to six zlotys a day. No one could give me even an approximate number of people employment on building sites in Tel Aviv, Jerusalem, or Haifa, the three biggest towns going through a construction boom, but the rough estimate is anything between 12,000 and 18,000. A great majority of them will move on to agriculture, but for now they are taking advantage of the building boom and saving for the future. At the current ratio of income to cost of living their saving potential is pretty good. And another thing helps—even those bricklayers-by-accident are aware, just like most workers in Palestine, of the cautionary example of American workers, who after years of economic good weather extended their consumption to their earning limits and found themselves utterly helpless when the crisis struck. The turnover of bricklayers here is pretty high, one young architect told me. Once they save enough, they move on to agriculture.

Unemployment is unheard of. On the contrary, there is a shortage of labor. A shortage, even though before the war Palestine started to show a tendency for reverse migration (when the old Zionist immigration is taken out of the equation, of course). Today Palestine is a typical immigrant country. During the busiest agricultural period, the schools have to send the upper years to work in the fields. That's a crisis *a rebours*. A shortage despite the availability of Arab workers, who may be as work-shy as the Spanish, but as cheap as Chinese coolies. A shortage despite the fact that the big orange groves, the *pardes*, need a lot of skilled manual labor. A shortage despite a well-regulated quota of labor immigration and an additional, fairly sizeable constant flow of "tourists" who come and then decide to stay for good. A shortage, even though in the last fourteen years the population of Haifa has doubled and the old Jewish quarter in Arab Jaffa has grown into a town of 60,000; while Jerusalem has acquired two populous new districts, the agro-colonies have turned into small towns, and a number of public works, mostly road building, are nearing completion.

Money seems plentiful. It's the first thought that comes to mind when seeing all these riches. A lot of capital. And yet, looking at the numbers, foreign capital has just only begun to wake up to the possibilities of this small country. So far, big international capital, mostly English, then American, has concentrated on the port of Haifa, Rutenberg Power Station, or the Dead Sea salinas. This capital works side by side with Jewish investment. Tel Aviv and Haifa, the two new industrial centers, have attracted only a small portion of it. In agriculture there is none. And yet, Palestine means agriculture. Palestine means plantations of oranges, which today are compared with the best in the world, and this is Jewish capital. The capital of powerful national institutions collecting money all over the world for the rebuilding of the spiritual home of all Jewry, plus private money donated by the more affluent local immigrants; there are very few big-time capitalists among them.

At first, one cannot shake off the impression that it is all a bit make-believe: after all, poverty is everywhere. France is chock-full of money and yet neighboring Syria is going through a very sharp crisis, just like Europe. Greece, Egypt, Turkey, and Transjordan too. Palestine feels like an oasis. A peculiar kind of ambition, a sort of "bet against all the odds" attitude, must have driven the Jews to such sacrifice and the creation of this phenomenon. Perhaps there some finely laid speculation trap for foreign capital, a humbug on a world scale? Well, let us take a closer look and see how much truth there is to it.

Palestine is an artificial creation—this is an undeniable fact. For decades it received a steady flow of investment, in money and human resources. People came here for an idea, just like they go to America for wealth. But the idea was followed by solid capital, given with noble intentions by rich magnates. Both people and money went there with no expectation of a quick return—at best, they thought it would be several times smaller than they could have got in other countries. It sounds odd, as if the nation that prides itself on its sense of commerce has simply, in this case, lost its sense. Palestine reborn, Eretz Israel, the Land of Israel, as it's called by the Jews, is an artificial creation. But it lives a real life.

The gold, which pulses in its veins, is pumped through two main arteries from the Diaspora—either the millions of small donations or the "pocket capital" brought into the country by the waves of immigrants. But gold flows into Palestine also as payment for the produce of its land. For what has been built in Palestine makes money. Noncommercial investments, unprofitable, made at the time when the best ventures one could hope for were sheep or wine, when no one even thought of this land's greatest treasure—oranges—all these investments turned out not only profitable but a runaway success. It is best illustrated by the price of land in the orange grove region: today one dunam is worth eighteen to forty Palestine pounds; a pound is worth thirty-two Polish zlotys; one dunam is a tenth of a hectare. Bearing in mind that it takes at least four years before an orange grove brings in first profits, the average price for a tenth of uncultivated (but with access to the precious water) land is between six and eight thousand zlotys. In spite of these prices, everyone wants to grow oranges.

The myth about Palestine being kept afloat by begging, by an artificial infusion of gold, collapses when confronted with such numbers. Today's Palestine ceased being dependent on the Diaspora long ago. Today, Palestine and the Diaspora work hand in hand in creating the Palestine of the future, which means expanding the Jewish portfolio of real estate. The crisis weakened the Diaspora's financial muscle, but it happened when, for the first time since antiquity, this country has become again a land flowing with milk and honey.

4

More Beautiful than Paris

"They say Tel Aviv is even more beautiful than Paris."

That's what I heard from a young Jewish student, who probably hadn't seen Paris, let alone Tel Aviv. Haifa—yes, that's a truly beautiful city. It will be a great port and still remain beautiful. The blue of the bay has been taken up by a long, narrow strip of land where the sea has been pushed out to make room for new concrete moorings, piers, and jetties—the new waterfront. Along that flat, gray strip on which, as in Polish Gdynia,[1] new depots and warehouses will rise, and small wagons loaded with cement needed for further expansion of the future port now trundle. But just behind it lies Old Arab Haifa, the Haifa of winding narrow streets and cul-de-sacs dotted with porticos of bijoux palaces; and the Haifa of sheep herded into town for the market day, now basking in the sun on the huge slabs, big as those laid in mosque courtyards. Further on, a new modern city has grown around it like an amphitheater, with the bay for an arena and the long ridge of Mount Carmel covered with olive groves and sabra for its surrounding wall. It looks as if the town undercuts the hill—it washes off more and more of its slope, covering it with climbing branches of streets which soon, instead of leaves, sprout a thick foliage of red and gray rooftops. But this assault on Mount Carmel, the mountain of Elijah and hermits, is not carried out merely at its foot. On its top, cutting through the groves of pines and cypresses, runs a new ring of tarmac road with wonderful views of the misty, faraway blue of the sea. Villas, small palaces, and sanatoria. It's hard to find a more varied urban space. Down below, on the coast, the metallic walls of cisterns call attention

---

1 Gdynia—Polish city and a major seaport on the coast of the Baltic Sea; when Poland regained independence 1918 and Gdańsk was given the status of "free city," it was decided to build a new port nearby in a small fishing village of Gdynia to serve the needs of the new state. (Transl.)

to the gigantic pipeline, which will soon start pumping from the rigs of Mosul, hundreds miles away, crude oil directly to the ships. Up above the lush districts of this garden city and their picturesquely scattered housing estates spread out. Bustling trade, signboards, shop windows, stalls, and street booths, instead of spreading around the whole of Haifa, are concentrated downtown, near the port, rarely venturing up the hill. In this town of huge commercial importance all trade seems to have been channeled into one enclosed neighborhood.

But Tel Aviv...

Someone in Poland wrote once that the town was cheap and tawdry. And so it is. An American journalist I met here told me he didn't like the town. An average, provincial American town, a typical "Made in the USA." He was right. I agreed with both opinions, and with many others, but.... There is something about this town, which is younger than the young students of its local universities, whose oldest building has lived to the grand old age of twenty-six. It is as if surrounded by a halo, an aura, something that makes one pronounce its name like a half-mythical city of wonders, like the word "spring" in a country short of water or "sun" under the polar night. Or to put it differently, Tel Aviv, the name of a young town not bigger than the Polish Katowice, Przemyśl, or Białystok, a town of cozy middle-class houses, small manufactures and shady boulevards, the name of this town without much of a yesterday, in the mouths of so many people, Jews and Arabs alike, sounds heroic, like Hastings, Tsushima, Jemappes, Olszynka Grochowska, or Radzymin.[2] I find the thought amusing, but nevertheless it is so. People talk about Tel Aviv as of a great victorious battle. And so it is too. The country, which has the unique city of Jerusalem, a country which has for its port wonderful Haifa, is simply infatuated with the town where the freshly poured tarmac is barely set and the mortar in its walls barely dry. An enigma.

* * *

This town of which people speak the way we speak of Kłuszyn[3] has nothing big about it. The longest streets are not long or wide enough for their perspective not to be cut short by the green of young trees. The new opera

---

2   Hastings, etc.... —names of towns associated with decisive battles that changed the course of history. (Transl.)

3   Kłuszyn—a village near Smolensk; in 1610, part of the Polish-Lithuanian Commonwealth where the Polish cavalry, the hussars, won a decisive battle against overwhelming Russian forces. (Transl.)

house is a beautiful building, but not monumental. The great synagogue is even smaller than the opera. But the trade unions are housed in a massive construction, which as far as aesthetics go, compares well with Kaiser Wilhelm's castle in Poznań, except it's a cheaper version of it and looks like a stage set. The only truly impressive building is the town hall and a dozen or so bigger but privately owned buildings. Generally, it's a town of mostly low buildings, several floors at most, but drowning in garden greenery. No plot can be fully built over. The gardens separate all the affordable new houses in Tel Aviv, and often feature a familiar sight of washing hung out to dry, just like it used to be "back in the country," in Kutno or Suwałki. Inside the homes one can still find old oil-painted illustrations and "embroideries," mostly showing Bible stories, just like "back in the country," but these are practically relics.

This town is like a big pyre set on fire on the seashore for all arriving Jews, from all the ghettos in the world, to throw their rags. Here one can still hear Yiddish, here Jews still speak among themselves in Polish, Russian, and German. Here too one can still see Jews of a kind seen often in the Diaspora— dirty, fearful, and with that melancholy which veils their faces when sunk in thought. Here the nation undergoes a great quarantine after twenty centuries of pauperdom. There is no Jew here who has not passed through Tel Aviv.

It's a quarantine of a peculiar kind. Instead of being put into isolated barracks, a man is simply thrown into the sea of life. He will not infect others, they will infect him with new life. All he does is walk around and look, before he even starts searching for work. He sees a town that has been built quickly like no other, or very few in the world. Where now stand banks, cinemas, and cafes, all that stood there in 1924, in Lord Allenby Street, named after the man who won Palestine from Turkey, were dunes. Even in later years, Montefiore Street was still covered by desert grass. In 1909, Tel Aviv was constituted as a town, the first in thousands of years built entirely, and lived in, by Jews. At that time the town population numbered 550. Jews from neighboring Arab Jaffa moved to the new town slowly and with reluctance. In 1919, the number rose to 3,000 and in three short years it rose again to 10,000. Today the town's population exceeds 50,000 and is still growing.

***

Meir comes from Białystok. What was he doing it Białystok? He was a carpenter, what else? It's his eighth year in Palestine. How is his life here? Good? Meir smiles, cunningly almost. Why wouldn't it be good? Isn't everybody's life good here? What is Meir the carpenter doing here? What is he doing? He is making cars!

Last year Nachum Sokołow arrived in Jerusalem. That Tel Aviv, what a wonderful city, he says. What growth, the industry built from scratch. And that car plant . . .

Gentlemen from the Zion executive looked at each other—What? How? Where? Ah, that little alley off Herzl Street. They went, they saw. Indeed. A big shed, eight Jews. Four carpenters, two upholsterers, a bookmaker, and a locksmith. Altogether a factory making coach bodies. Buses are the main means of transport in Palestine. Jews hit on the great idea of importing just engines and chassis and manufacturing the bodies on-site. They had a little capital, borrowed some more, and their first three buses put them in profit.

* * *

What was Nalewki[4] like before the war? Hundreds of little workshops squeezed into backyards, attics, and basements. Those were the microcapitalists, suppliers of goods to the Russian colossus. That Russia is gone and the workshops look forlorn.

Tel Aviv has its own Nalewki, but it's different—green, clean, and sunny. And it's the Nalewki of a different kind of Jew. But here too are little workshops supplying the colossus of the Levant. Faraway, in Manchester and Birmingham, inside the quiet cabinets of big business, bosses anxiously follow reports explaining the reasons for the retreat of the great British dreadnoughts of trade and industry. Have the Arabs followed in the footsteps of India? Has the Soviet intrigue cut off communication with those markets? A crisis?

These questions seriously worry those big bosses and their price-dumping and competition specialists. They have run many victorious campaigns, they have more adversaries on their boards than the German flying ace Baron von Richthofen scored hits in air combat. Now this market is being pulled away from under their feet, the proud empire has just shrunk, by about the size of the Levant. The Tel Aviv Nalewki has emerged as a worthy competitor of British big business. Each annual report confirms its advance. The microcapitalists of the small workshops undercut the colossus. That's Meir's Tel Aviv.

Neither of Meir's sons live in Tel Aviv. One is currently employed on the road near Tel Hai; the second, as of the first of next month, will start as manager

---

4   Nalewki—a street in Warsaw and a Jewish neighborhood in prewar Warsaw. (Transl.)

of a drainage works somewhere up in the north of the country on newly acquired land. "They both know manual work," says Meir. And he says it the way he might have said back in Poland that they "both served in the Legions."[5] I remember that the previous day I spoke with an official from a certain ministry in Poland, a Jew, who was telling me about his nephew here in Tel Aviv—"Can you imagine, he is a simple worker here!" Meir is a craftsmen, but, with all that, also a speculator; a typical Nalewki capitalist. Meir speaks of his sons and their manual work, giving me to understand—"My family is good stock, myself, not so much." Meir paid for his sons' education, including university. Back in Białystok he was proud of his sons and was telling his neighbors, like he probably does now: "My sons—oh, they are clever. They will be doctors, barristers. Surely, they won't end up like me, ordinary workers."

Meir is an old man now. Old people don't change. But Meir still has not forgotten his Białystok dream. He speaks about the road on which his son (the "barrister") literally broke stones, as though it was his doctoral thesis. Old people don't change. The nature of nations does not change. Two thousand years instilled in Jews a contempt for manual labor. Meir did not go to work on the roads. Nor did he go to work the land. He stayed in town. Yet he looks on his sons, those manual laborers, as on superior social material. It is the better part of himself. We talk about Palestinian industry. I tell him how I admire their commercial sense, how I like to see the poor Nalewki Jews fight their victorious battle against British concerns and trusts. That here will rise the greatest industrial center of the biggest continent. That it will be making money, big money . . . like Morgan, Rothschild. . . .

Meir smiles again, but now a beaming and playful smile, like a child expecting a nice surprise. Does he see behind my words the road to a Rothschild-like fortune? No. Meir takes me by the wrist of my hand, his eyes a-twinkle: "You know, just behind Bet Hanan, there is a lovely *pardes* there. All it needs is a house. . . . "

A *pardes* . . .

---

5   The Legions—Legiony Polskie: name for a Polish military force formed many times during the Polish history of struggle for independence, beginning with the Napoleonic Wars and throughout the nineteenth century; Legiony Polskie were established in August 1914 in Galicia at the beginning of World War I; the Legions became a founding myth for the creation of modern Poland. (Transl.)

* * *

Man's dreams change here. . . . But there is also a young generation that grew up together with Tel Aviv, whose parents are the town's patricians now. The poet Bialik is joined by a whole legion of Jewish intelligentsia in creating new cultural life and bringing it to Eretz Israel.

The German salon culture, somewhat heavy and dour, is slowly broken up from within by the local southern temperament. Music dominates social life. I'm not a connoisseur but I feel that music in today's Palestine plays the same role as theatre in ancient Greece, *corrida* in Spain, or cafés in Vienna. Interest in the new Hebrew literature is as strong as the new Ukrainian literature is among the young intelligentsia in Ukraine. The point is to spread and popularize the Hebrew language. Which is quite successful. Everything is in Hebrew, and Yiddish spurned, even banned, like the Polish language under the partitions.[6] A Yiddish newspaper is unthinkable. It would be boycotted, or more than boycotted even. The Hebrew language is another measure which I can use in this book to showcase the achievements of the new Palestine. For now, suffice it to say that Latin was still a living language when Hebrew was already dead. Mussolini, who tries at any price to revive ancient Rome in Italy, boasts great success in this field. But the revival of Latin would be considered a fantasy, an impossible dream. Yet the revival of Hebrew is a fact.

"More beautiful than Paris." Those words came back to me one evening when strolling down Allenby Street towards the beach. It was a Sabbath evening. On the Sabbath everything stops, even buses. The evening is holy. And that day, it seemed, doubly holy. Outside coffee shops, spilling onto the smooth tarmac of the roads and lit by electric light, people danced in the streets.

The joy of the Jewish street in Warsaw, or elsewhere, has for me more the character of a nervous spasm, rackety and tiresome. It's what they call "veritable *heder*."[7] Here it was like people had no room in their homes and had come outside to have fun in open space, where dancing is easier. Street dancing here seemed to be a simple natural urge, like nowhere else. From out of a big coffee shop on the corner, with walls the color of amber but called Sapphire, came the strains of a *hora*, a group dance, like ballet, but whose roots go back to antiquity.

---

6   Partitions of Poland—between 1772–1795, the Polish-Lithuanian Commonwealth was apportioned among its more powerful neighbors—Austria, Russia, and Prussia—in three successive partitions, which ended Poland's existence as a state; sovereign Poland and Lithuania remerged only 123 years later at the end of World War I. (Transl.)

7   *Heder* (Heb.: "room")—traditional Jewish elementary school. (Transl.)

Hora now filled the whole street and the town, spilling onto the beaches with their brightly lit cafes, with open-air dancing under the star-studded sky. The spasm of Jewish joy in the Diaspora, the noisy racket of our small provincial towns, dissolved here into rhythm and balmy weather. A Jew, who even in the most Jewish of towns could not but feel a stranger, here feels he has every right, including legal, to feel at home. That's the enigma of Tel Aviv, that's why Tel Aviv is to Jews what it is. The longing for home drove the superfast construction of Tel Aviv. The Jew is looking at it now through the joy of fulfilling his dream, through the joy of seeing the end of his wandering. Tel Aviv, the Ancient Hill of Spring,[8] is more beautiful than Paris.

---

8   The name "Tel Aviv" can be translated from Hebrew as "Ancient Hill of Spring." (Transl.)

5

The Jews Who Do Not Like It Here

When I arrived in Tel Aviv for the first time, it was midday; at 4 p.m., I was at the Polish consulate, and by 6 I was being driven in the consul's car to visit neighboring colonies surrounding the city like a wreath. As I wrote before, in Palestine one feels from the start that this new Palestine, the true Palestine, lies not in towns but in the country, the *pardes* orchards, Samaria, Tiberias, Emek. Everything else is just as old Meir used to say: "Myself, I'm nothing, but my sons laying down the roads—now, that's the true people." When I learned that the consul and another Polish official from some ministry were going to Petah Tikva, the famous old colony, I hitched a lift with them. And we were joined in the car by an elegant beautiful woman, a true lady.

The elegant lady is from Warsaw. Her husband is a leading doctor or a lawyer, who arrived in Tel Aviv, in the "homeland," eight months earlier. I ask the lady a few questions, but after a while it is me who answers questions. How is Warsaw? Adria? Banda? Can't be—Ordonka is really coming here too?[1] I only read *Wiadomości Literackie*. Do you really know Mr. Grydzewski?[2] But

---

1   Ordonka—Hanka Ordonówna (born Maria Anna Pietruszyńska, 1902–1050), Polish singer, dancer, and actress, regarded as the greatest star in prewar Poland; in 1931, she married Count Michał Tyszkiewicz, who wrote many of her songs. She died in Beirut. (Transl.)
2   Grydzewski—Mieczysław Grydzewski (b. Grützhändler, 1894–1970), Polish Jewish journalist, founder of literary magazines *Skamander* and *Wiadomości Literackie*, which shaped and influenced the literary scene of prewar Poland. (Transl.)

not Krzywicka?[3] Have you any new Polish books? The last thing I read was *Zazdrość i medycyna*. . . . [4]

The lady is planning to spend next winter in Poland. What's carnival like here? Yes, it's true, it's lovely. An interesting sight, this universal joy, the noise, the dancing. Very interesting. Once I even danced with an Arab. A very cultured, elegant Arab. But Warsaw, ah . . .

The car sped down the smooth tarmac road as if sliding on ice. We left the suburbs behind us and now on both sides of the road we were passing rows of orange trees, a lane of two-meter-high trees on thin trunks supporting a thick wall of very green leaves. It was like a sea of green, an impenetrable thicket, like a steppe. Here and there above the trees flashed a red roof. Then the road turned onto an alley lined with cypresses, which brought us into a small town.

"What's this?" asked the lady.

"Petah Tikva."

"Ah, so this is Petah Tikva."

It was not the official from the ministry asking, nor was it me: it was the elegant Jewish lady from Tel Aviv. Now we were surprised. Petah Tikva lies so close to Tel Aviv that it is impossible not to know it. It would be like not knowing Wilanów in Warsaw or Werki in Vilnius.[5] Even more so because this colony has behind it a whole legend of heroic deeds, struggle, and sacrifice, a legend whose last pages were written down after the Arab attacks of 1928. It is my first day in Tel Aviv and I'm already on my way to Petah Tikva, a place which only a week ago I knew nothing about. I am a Pole born and bred, the lady is Jewish and has lived here for eight months. It is her first venture outside Tel Aviv. She is telling us about it with such nonchalance, as if she doesn't give a fig about what is actually happening here.

Our surprise shows and it calls for some more explanations. The lady tells us that she feels very little connection with all this business here. She is not a Zionist and even baulks at the idea of being "reduced exclusively to one nationality." She feels European, yes, just so—European. Warsaw, yes, she loves Warsaw, our Warsaw! Here things are not just utterly new, they are raw, and so narrow-minded. Take the Sabbath. Can you imagine that on Saturday I cannot

---

3 Krzywicka—Irena Krzywicka (1899–1994), Polish Jewish journalist, writer, and translator; one of Poland's first modern feminists and promoter of sex education. (Transl.)

4 *Jealousy and Medicine* (Warsaw: Gebethner i Wolf, 1933)—a popular novel in prewar Poland by Michał Choromański. (Transl.)

5 Wilanów . . . Werki—beautiful royal and aristocratic palatial complexes near large cities in prewar Poland. (Transl.)

buy anything. Not a sausage. On Friday evening they proclaim the holiday, just as they do in our dirty provincial towns. But even there I can shop both on Saturdays and Sundays. Here—nothing.

We are walking around the colony while the ministry official carries out his important ministerial assignment at Petah Tikva's council. From the dusty and provincial-looking main square we move down into an alley of small houses covered with ivy. In front of the houses, instead of Polish mallows stand stubby coco palms and orange trees. The lady prattles on. She would never like to live here—alright, that villa with a veranda looks pretty and the neighborhood well off even, but still—it's the back of beyond. Sure, an 8,000-strong colony may laugh at the Arabs, but still. . . . And that silence. . . . That palatable absence of our European life. . . .

And she admits she simply does not understand. She does not understand those young people with university diplomas who go and break stones for the roads, who choose to bury their youths in some "collective" ("What's it called? A kibbutz? Oh, you know that already?") . . . yes, in some "kibbutz" in the Jordan Valley, when no one was forcing them. And then such a kibbutznik, a young man, before he knows it, becomes a father of three kids. Yes, truly. Perhaps you can call it heroism, perhaps it makes an interesting story for a journalist, perhaps without them there would be just sand and desert here. . . . But, then, would it be such a tragedy if there were?

You are wrong, dear reader, completely, if you think, "Ah, this is the kind a woman who thinks herself too precious, a birdbrain, a doll." But no, not at all. She was simply the kind of person who had a very sensible approach to life, life which should bring the greatest possible material pleasures at the least material cost. Hers was a case of a straightforward bourgeois rationale. I am not saying this with disdain, nor with undue emphasis. Her opinions were not that different from the opinions of highly cultured people. The story of people who went to build roads and drain swamps instead of living off their parents' money, or taking a pretty wife with a nice dowry, or even spending their youth working hard to make their fortunes later—such people, if noticed, would certainly raise a few eyebrows, even those of Petronius, the smartest, noblest *arbiter elegantiarum* of them all.[6]

---

6 Petronius—a character in Henryk Sienkiewicz's novel *Quo Vadis* (Warszawa: Gebethner i Wolf, 1896) about the early years of Christianity in ancient Rome. The novel won Sienkiewicz the Nobel Prize for Literature in 1905. (Transl.)

* * *

In Tel Aviv I met a young doctor, a shy man, who also travelled on the *Dacia*, except that he was in second not fourth class. I asked him what he had seen so far. It turned out that in those two weeks he had seen very little, just Tel Aviv. He explained to me that he did not come as a tourist, but to settle here, open his practice, and earn money.

But he felt rather unsettled and insecure here. More: he felt lost, alienated. His job hunting was slow and unsuccessful. Palestine, a country the size of the Vilnius region, had perhaps too few workers, but as far as the working intelligentsia was concerned (i.e. those not working on the roads), they were in plentiful supply. They will not find work as easily as bricklayers. Jerusalem University is open, but of the departments functioning in practical sense (producing young lawyers, doctors, philologists, etc.) there is only one of medicine, and the arrival of a lot of young graduates with diplomas has easily satisfied the relatively modest needs of the country. I tried to cheer him up by telling him he would soon find work, but after a while didn't know what else to tell him. "Well, this is your country," I said.

The young doctor looked at me, then fell silent. The thing is, he does not feel it's his country. He never dreamed or longed for Palestine. He does not think of it as his homeland. The patch of land where one was born and knows everyone and has lived for a long time—yes, that's one's homeland. But a faraway land—no. He does not consider it bad or wrong. On the other hand, one can love one's religion or social class (I didn't get the impression he loved either). In the small Galician town, where he opened his first practice, he didn't fare well. Oversupply of doctors. He came here. "You can't imagine how awful I feel here, how terribly alienated."

He studied in Lwów.[7] There were antisemitic skirmishes when students formed lanes, pushing and pulling Jews along and beating them with sticks. My doctor cried out, "I'm not a Jew! I consider myself Polish!" landing a big whack on his head in reply. His Jewish friends heard his cry, and some of them even tossed him into the laughing crowd, carried away with the joy of beating fellow men. His friends—he knew them—they believed him. He did not. In Berlin, he would have cried—"I'm a German!"

---

7   Lwów—Pol.; Rus.: Lvov; Ukr.: Lviv—a city in Galicia in the eastern part of Lesser Poland Province in prewar Poland, now in Western Ukraine. (Transl.)

"You are surprised, probably, and think I'm an opportunist. Well, so be it: you have never been in the position of someone beaten up because of the blood in his veins."

Since that day, he continued, a wall has grown between him and his other Jewish friends. The assimilated Jews knew he did not believe his affirmation of Polishness; the Zionists scorned him even more. With Jews who thought like him he did not get on anyway. Today he is in Palestine. Palestine is the dream of a great many people in Poland, Romania, all over the world, of thousands of new *halutzim*. He is here. And he feels foreign.

"I'm simply honest with you. You are an outsider, you observe and you go away. You understand that someone may not think of loving a country or a religion. The main thing I picked up from all that talk about Palestine, what I heard and understood, was that there was a boom. People are building, ploughing, draining swamps; they work, hurry, and have no time or care to ask you what you think or don't think. Well, not about your origins, anyway. Here, people quarrel and fight each other, yet they think alike. I don't think like them. Should I pretend? It's hard, and I don't even know how to pretend. At least for now."

We had a long chat. He spoke about the invisible dictatorship of Zionism. How Yiddish is being shunned and discriminated against, how the presses of a Yiddish newspaper would be smashed to pieces, how during Passover one is forbidden to eat bread, only unleavened matzah, and when a liberal bakery put bread in its window the workers ("please note, sir—workers!—socialists!") they made a great hullabaloo about it and burnt the bread on the street as if it were a provocation. Yes, sir, it's a dictatorship. Just like in Italy, like in Russia.

At which point the doctor concluded: "Dictatorship is the child of an idea."

I said: "Except perhaps for Christianity?"

The doctor thought and replied: "Yes. With religions, dictatorship is a youthful phase."

* * *

In my mind, those two are always together. They are the only people I met in Palestine who disliked Palestine. And I went out of my way to meet many different people here. I think that all the unhappy people here are of this kind. For to feel at home here, or feel like it is a paradise on earth (and I met people who felt just that) it's not enough to have a "leave of entry" certificate and 1,000 pounds cash, or even come as a tourist and just stay—one has also to be driven by a Zionist dream.

It's simple and clear as day: if it weren't for this idea, this country would not exist. The following example will make this clear: if there were no ideal of independence, Warsaw would still exist and people would live in it. If there were no Zionism, its call to Jewry to return its fatherland, there would be no Tel Aviv. More, there would be no Petah Tikva, or Rishon LeZion, or Magdiel, not even Emek Israel—none of those rich, picturesque colonies would exist: just the desert, swamps, and malaria. And that is why almost nothing here has been built by business, or at least the overwhelming majority of it; it has been driven into existence by an idea, an idea which is omnipresent, like the presence of the One who always manifest Himself in the deeds of His people, the biblical Yahveh of Israel.

6

The Onward March of Israel

In year the 1882, when the first group of immigrants founded the first Palestinian colony, the movement of return to the land of the forefathers still functioned without any organizational form. The tens of years that followed were a truly Sisyphean effort to work that land. Arabs, the Turkish administration, the foreign climate, malaria, and poverty are all woven together into old stories from those times. Half a century later, the colony blossoms in riches, and yet even today the official publications of this far from modest nation proclaim without any hesitation that there was a time when but a single man saved the Zionist project from collapsing. And no, it's not Herzl's name that those publications mention first. Even the Palestinian socialists pronounce his name, surname, and title with reverence—Baron Edmund de Rothschild.

There were few colonies then. They vegetated without money or men; malaria scared them all—whole generations were dying off. To get rid of malaria, the swamps had to be drained and replanted with water-extracting eucalyptus. Not only were people scarce, but money too. And that came from Rothschild. He generated the first wave of gold, the gold of the big capitalists and philanthropists like himself, but also the gold of the millions of small donations collected in Jewish houses all over the world. With him also came organization.

In 1901 Rothschild transferred his Palestinian undertaking and its founding capital to the ICA (the Jewish Colonization Association; today, the PICA— the Palestine Jewish Colonization Association), which in Lower Galilee set up Kfar Tabor, Yavnil, Sedera, and two other colonies. As a big fund purchasing land from the Arabs, it works arm in arm with another financial colossus, the famous Keren Keyemet LeYisrael—the Jewish National Fund. Out of its own pockets it still buys land and, working alongside Rothschild's capital, has created the new colonies of Ben Shemen, Hulda, Kineret, Degania Alef ("The First"), Merhavia.

After the war, this pair was joined by a third institution Keren Hayesod—the Founding Fund—formed in April 1929. While the mission of the first two was to buy land for the colonists, the third's is to provide settlers with tools and livestock. In fact, it broadly serves "the economic and cultural development of Palestine" and is present in all walks of life.

These organizations, with their multimillions, were necessary for the survival of Palestine. Only here, in situ, can one see why no progress would have been possible without them Palestine is a classic example of how great things can be achieved through a combination of big money and the right people. And how to invest in a "loss-leader." Here, land purchase cannot proceed in any other way but on a huge scale; individual Jewish settlements among Arabs would be madness. In my country, land is bought and then ploughed. In Palestine, one cannot give one dunam of land to agriculture without first draining and improving it. And thus, of the land acquired by Keren Kayemet, two-thirds had to be improved. It is a back-to-front and upside-down approach—land has to drained before being irrigated. Only farmers can fully understand what it means for a small landowner, what it means for a *halutz*—a pioneer settler—when, like a tank clearing the field before an advancing soldier, two machines like the PICA and Keren Kaymet first move in, conquering for him (literarily, though in a peaceful way) the land, followed by Keren Hayesod that equips him with buildings, livestock, and all the necessary inventory.

That is how the new Israel marches on. Starting from the sea. Some thirty kilometers south of Jaffa a more or less solid stretch of settlement begins. It is the richest part of Palestine, the *pardes* region, and it is mostly privately owned. It circles around Tel Aviv and climbs up through Petah Tikva and Herzliya towards French Syria. There are more and more tracts of land bought not just by private capital but also by the National Fund, Keren Kayemet. From Wadi Harawat the huge 43,000 dunam latifundium of Keren Kayemet begins. A group of private colonies has grown around the rich Hadera, but a little further up it changes into PICA land. And then, next to Haifa, private capital is neighboring onto Keren, which has acquired the terrain between Haifa and Acre, where the expansion of the new port promises a good future for the investment. There, the march from the sea stops.

But at this highest northernmost point it takes a turn southeast and unfurls as a massive, 164,000 dunam tract of land, the most important part of the new Palestine—the Valley of Israel. Emek Israel reaches all the way to the

Jordan Valley, where further to the north, around Tiberias and beyond, lie the old Rothschild and Kayemet colonies. These are the farthest outposts of Israel, her islands. A number of smaller *kibbutzim* scattered south of Tel Aviv towards Jerusalem rounds up the inland march of Jewish settlement in Palestine.

How much did it all cost? It's hard to calculate the cost, even in money. The powerful, private colonization aside, one would have to collate and add up the costs of the acquisition and then amelioration of the lands owned by Keren Kayemot and Keren Hayesod, which are £2,004,733 and £4,669,547, respectively. Other organizations, such as the health service Hadassa, which invested a million and a half, we shall leave aside too, just like the Rothschild funds with their different kinds of long-term investments set to bring different kinds of benefits. British statistics, excellent as they are, do not give the full picture of the invested sums. Besides, Palestine (being indeed an excellent investment opportunity) tries to show herself even more attractive than it is. Therefore I would rather not speak about things I haven't checked or analyzed personally and which, in this country growing before my very own eyes, would be outdated in a few months anyway.

7

Suppliers of Men and Money

Before departing for Palestine I was informed that the country was a quite important export market for Polish products. I was amazed to hear that our textiles from Bielsko can seriously—and quite successfully too—compete with British products. And not just from Bielsko, but from Łódź and Białystok. A Jew arriving from Poland (emigration from Russia, forbidden in the USSR, is now a thing of the past, but ten years ago it was huge) simply does not know English materials but knows and is used to ours. The success of our textile industry can be confirmed perhaps by the fact that a newly established factory in Tel Aviv bears the oddly non-Hebrew name of Lodzia. And so the push to increase our export to Palestine continues. As usual, the favored industry takes a leading position ahead of agriculture, although the importance of the latter as the foundation of our economy is slowly beginning to dawn on some people. I was earnestly assured that our potatoes and timber would be in great demand here (Vilnius take note!). In practice, however, those here asking about our potatoes will be handed a brochure advising them that potatoes are more successfully grown at home, while the best foreign import is chemical fertilizer. I can picture the surprise of our foreign trade bureaucrats when they see that people here do not buy our potatoes and import fertilizer from Chile, not Chorzów.[1] Never mind. Still, Poland alongside other countries with a large Jewish population, remains an important exporter of both men and money.

In the eyes of the *yishuv* (the Jewish settlement in Palestine) all countries in the world fall into one of two types: suppliers of men and suppliers of money. Of course, some routes of supply have already been well established: some

---

1   Chorzów—a city in the industrial district of Upper Silesia, incorporated into Poland in 1922 following three uprisings; it contained a big nitrogen factory producing fertilizers. (Transl.)

countries traditionally provide men, others capital. And of course, no single country supplies only settlers and another only money. These two commodities are managed and directed by big organizations and are judiciously delivered to all parts of the country just where they are needed most. The classic supplier of men is Poland; of money, the United States.

People often talk about the Polish Jewish conflict of interests. This book in not the place to go into a long, or even short, discussion of the problem. But I do think that even the worst antisemite convinced of the harm inflicted by Jews on Poland cannot deny that, as far as Palestine is concerned, there is no conflict. Even if he assumes that Jews are an undesired element in Poland, he should greet with satisfaction the fact that of all Diaspora countries Poland has the strongest emigration movement and the weakest when it comes to export of capital.

In the years since the establishment of the Mandate, Polish immigrants have made up the highest proportion of the total of world Jewry settling in Palestine—39.8 percent or over 50,000 people. This is not a large percentage of the three million Jews living in Poland, but it is quite a lot given the size of Palestine and the very tight immigration controls imposed by the British authorities. At any rate it's not a *quantité négligeable* at a time when unemployment among the working class and young intelligentsia in Poland is painfully high—and when we also realize that most of those emigrating are young people, quite poor, the *halutzim* who bring to Palestine not much more than their youthful enthusiasm and hands itching for work.

When it comes to the export of capital, from the first on the world list Poland drops to fifth. After us comes Romania and then the countries where the Jewish Diaspora is relatively small—Czechoslovakia and the Netherlands. People in Poland often make a point about the wealth of our three million Jews. But that three million mass of Polish Jewry, among whom the Zionist influence is undeniable, since 1919 has sent to Palestine, by way of donations to Keren Hayesod, £217,999 or 6,976,048 Polish zlotys. For a sum collected over eleven years (the statistics come from 1931), it is not really such a great fortune. Of course, apart from these official donations there is also private capital that has emigrated together with the emigrants, but there are no statistics for that. Nevertheless, these figures show something. The United States, with its Jewish population almost as big as the Polish one, in the same period of time sent to Palestine 23.5 times fewer people and eleven times more money.

These are the figures, quite apart from a joke that for every Polish Jew arriving in Palestine two are going back. And the legend about the billions being sucked out of Poland to Palestine. The actual export to Palestine, where without the Zionist settlers there would be no market for Polish products, is worth more than those "billions."

* * *

Keren Kayemet and Keren Hayesod, active over many years in what was a relatively small and poor country, turned it before our eyes into a country of great possibilities. They managed their capital, giving priority to noncommercial investment over a purely financial calculations and, as a result, apart from a private capital fund, built a socio-philanthropic one—one of such immense influence it is impossible to compare them with any other philanthropic organizations in the world.

That philanthropic capital has had one great advantage over the basically nonexistent private capital here in that all those private colonies have grown out of loans and mortgages. Yet, today's Palestine has a fairly large chunk of land under Jewish settlement, which exists and functions quite independently of any outside support. The Palestine of the collectives and the *halutzim* lives side by side with the Palestine of the old colonies. It is time to take a closer look at them.

8

Malaria and Millions

X, whose guest I am at one of the oldest Palestinian colonies Petah Tikva, which we have already discussed, is without a doubt one of the richest private Jewish settlers. He arrived here before the war, part of the wave which flowed out of Russia with the rise of antisemitism and pogroms. He spoke a lot about the hard years of war and Arab attacks in which his young son was killed; less about what really interests me—what life is like here now. I heard the same yesterday in Rehovot, the same in Ness Ziona, and basically the same in all the private colonies. These people know that if the world is talking about Palestine as a land free of economic crises they are mentioned as that country's rich. And they talk about their riches with reluctance.

The outskirts of Petah Tikva are mostly covered by small houses; my host's abode is a large villa. It does not have much of an orchard, nor even a vegetable garden. Instead, behind one of the walls spreads an orange grove. The colonist X is the owner of some 400 dunams. In Poland this would be a small estate of forty hectares, its owner would not have the means to send his children to a good school. One dunam here—established and profitable—goes for £150. Our colonist's estate is thus worth £60,000 or over 2,000,000 Polish zlotys.

My host pleads with me not to mention him by name and he tries to give me as little information as he possibly can. But still: he tells me his son studied in one of Berlin's polytechnics, his daughter recently returned from her studies in the West; indeed she speaks very good French. We look over the neighbor's land. A very nice *pardes*, I say. My host informs me it is for sale, but adds, "Well, what can he get for it, poor man, for his seventy dunams. . . ? Twelve thousand pounds . . . ?" Twelve thousand pounds! I haven't heard the richest Polish landowners speak about this kind of money with such nonchalance! Then he asks about the price of land in Volhynia.[1] I can't give him exact figures, but soon we calculate that he could easily afford several thousand morgens.[2] Our colonist concludes with satisfaction that he would be "as grand a lord as count Potocki." Alas, he can't remember very well which of Potocki's Ukrainian estates he has in mind. On second thoughts he reflects that perhaps "not as big as that." But remembering the current worth of our landed gentry, I assure him that actually he would be bigger than that. Apparently, he has long lost touch with all Volhynian realities for he thinks I'm making fun of him.

He belongs to that interesting type of prewar colonists who have already made it. The type perhaps not dissimilar to the early American colonists whose mentality was shaped by the hardships of the early years and the riches they finally achieved. They are, shall we say, parsimonious. The younger generation spends freely and has needs just like the wealthy youth in the West. These men are not like that. They do show satisfaction, however, and claim that they came to this sandy wasteland driven by an idea, against all reason, and that now it has turned out they were a thousand times wiser than their cousins and friends who remained behind in Soviet Ukraine. But there is also certain hardness about them. Each *pardes* employs over a dozen, sometimes tens, of workers, attending to a few hundred trees, which need watering, weeding, and pruning. It is skilled gardening work rather than agrarian labor, and it has become an area of tension. Apart from the young *halutzim*, who later move on and take over their own land, there are Arabs, with much lower expectations in terms of wages. The older generation tended to employ Arab workers. That, however, proved to be untenable in the long run: Zionist public opinion strongly objected to such arrangements, as they slowed down and limited the influx of a Jewish workforce to Palestine. This also gave rise to another problem—lower wages for the Jewish workers. At the time of my stay at Petah Tikva, this was the reason—though others claim not the only one—for a strike.

Yet, to say that Jewish colonies employ only Arabs while the Jews are only rich landowners would be a myth. I have visited most of the bigger settlements, I have driven up and down the country by bus and by car, crossed it on foot, seen with my own eyes a dozen private farms, and I can confirm that the majority of the workforce is Jewish. The Arab workers are, of course, universally

---

1   Volhynia—a historic region currently situated between southeastern Poland, southwestern Belarus and Western Ukraine, but before World War II mostly part of Poland. (Transl.)

2   Morgen—a unit of measurement of land area in Northern Europe, of varying size, but by the end of the nineteenth century fixed at 2500 sqm or one quarter hectare. (Transl.)

present, most commonly along the border of Jewish territories, but everywhere there is a mixture of both elements. In the towns as well.

* * *

During the evening, X spins yarns about the old days. My own roots in the Ukrainian borderlands perhaps helped bring us closer together. One story was about Petah Tikva. It was the first among the early colonies set up in Palestine. In 1878, the first eight colonists arrived. Petah Tikva—the Gate of Hope—was founded on a sandy hill. All around it there was nothing. A mile away, barely standing, are the ruins of the old castle—Crusader or the Saracen—Ras el Ein; further still, an Arab village sitting on the ruins of Antipatris, where the Romans held Saint Paul prisoner and which was in the capital of the Crusaders' feudal territory in the Middle Ages. Now all is ruins. Everywhere below—swamps. Huge malarial marshes. But what the colonists feared most were Arab attacks. Yet the Arabs did not attack. They came, inspected the tents, and by the time they left they already had a name for the colonists—*Wlat el din*—Children of Death. Over a year later, on the hill named Gate of Hope, there was no one left. Only small piles of stones marking graves. Malaria.

Petah Tikva, however, lived on in the thoughts of the new settlers. Two years later, there were more of them. They settled, but this time the Arabs' attitude was less peaceful. They started attacking. No one went out to work in the fields on their own or unarmed. They kept watch nightly by the fire. By day they drained the swamps. They worked hurriedly, feverishly. Malaria added new stones to the line of old forgotten graves. Malaria, and now some other deadly illness, today known only from old stories.

Malaria won again. Children died first. Followed by weak women and men. At the end, there were only two men left alive. But they stayed. They stopped working on the swamps; they were too weak. They just sat there and wrote letters to Jaffa, pleading for more colonists. Just like dispatches from the frontline asking for reinforcements. They waited longer than soldiers would normally wait on the front. In vain. Sometime in 1886, the last survivor left the Gates of Hope on foot.

Then, not long afterwards, another wave of pogroms in Russia sent a new group of Jewish colonists to Palestine. In Jerusalem, they were told about Petah Tikva. They were ready to go. They were warned about malaria and the previous two attempts. But the people who had survived Russian pogroms were not scared by malaria. They went. The story goes that while some were still pitching camp, the rest were already digging ditches towards Ras el Ein.

The battle against the swamps went on for a few more years. The defeat of the third Petah Tikva was still a distinct possibility. Children died as before. At first, the Arabs looked with detached indifference at these strange people who kept returning to the empty marshes, shrouded at night in the mist, the "white sheet of death." But the Russian Jews were a tough, resilient people. They did not die. Instead, they called on more of their fellow countrymen who could not find a better place for themselves. The marshes were being pushed further and further away. Then they started planting orange trees. And the only threat left was Arab attacks. In the evenings, red lights flickering in the fields and on the red dunes near Antipatris, in Ras el Ein, marked the border of their settlements, from which—as they grew in numbers, white houses, and green trees—they watched the intruders apprehensively. Petah Tikva had conquered.

* * *

I was told that story by a man who had no talent for story telling whatsoever. I listened to this tale of a nation, whose history, religion, politics, and race felt foreign to me, but which by a strange twist of fate was woven into the fabric of my country. The management of that very same colony did not greet me in a friendly way. But by now, I have got used to seeing these people in different moods.

We had just come out on the main square and were waiting for the bus to Tel Aviv. The work in the fields done, the town center was full of people. Nothing looked like it might have looked in the old days, those old days. One could easily have concluded that the whole story was some kind of a bad dream. And yet, just now I suddenly felt like an archaeologist who had stumbled upon a forgotten fragment of some unknown epic.

9

Histadrut Haovdim

On the white wall of the house opposite, the afternoon sun is cutting out sharp silhouettes of palm trees. "*Sotsialisticheskoe stroitel'stvo. Podgotovka. Dvizhenie. Kollektivnye khoziaistva. Bor'ba klassov. Voprosy. Trudiashchiisia mir.*"[1] Hard, alien, and raw these words from Bolshevik Russia sound. A young man behind a desk spreads out his arms in a gesture of a rally speaker, savoring the music. Across my mind, as I'm bent over my notes, flits the thought that just like Latin became the language of science, French the language of the aristocracy, so this new Russian has become international—if not a language, then certainly an argot of socialism and its elites. Two Poles, one Latvian journalist, a Romanian socialist activist, and an American have arrived here from Russia—we're all gathered together to listen to a report on the building of socialist Palestine. Our speaker unveils before us all the splendors of that least known of Palestines. He is not one of those nervous communist agitators, afraid that at any moment he could be arrested by the police while an "inspector" from Minsk discovers thousands of zlotys "diverted for private use" from party funds, or a grumpy old man pushed out of his cushy job at a sick benefit society; we are not listening to a young, confident Komsomol snob, certain that his communist beliefs come with an iron-clad indemnity simply by virtue of his being a member of some hurrah-patriotic nation-building organization. This young man radiates the pure joy of doing work he deeply believes in, creation right here and right now; his words throb with the conviction of an ex cathedra delivery, the cathedra here being a great power in his country—the dangerous,

---

1 Rus.: "Socialistic construction industry. Preparation. Motions. Collective farming. Class struggle. Questions. Proletarian world." (Transl.)

blessed, and mighty Palestinian Workers Organization, colloquially known by the first two words of its name: the Histadrut Haovdim.

Out of 200,000 Jews living in Palestine, 45,000 are workers. In other words, a quarter of the country is working class. Out of those 45,000, 37,000 belong to the Histadrut Haovdim. But the Histadrut Haovdim is not just a trade union. It has developed into a very interesting organization, whose working method closely resembles that of an American trust. Just like an American trust, which buys the portfolio of a company, de facto taking it over, leaving it a degree of independence, but making sure it protects its interest, the Histadrut Haovdim either creates dependent union structures or takes over already existing ones. Along with Histadrut Haovdim, a huge dairy and poultry cooperative Tnuva has developed, which controls all the trade in these commodities and has divided the country into administrative districts with its central office in Tel Aviv. It has by now branched out into foreign trade dealing in honey, vegetables, fruit jams, etc. Their turnover for 1924 was £22,000. Two years ago, it came to £147,000.

The Histadrut also controls the Agrarian Bank, with a founding capital of £110,000, as well as educational and cultural organizations, the sick benefit society, the department for social housing, a sports organization Hapoel, and, finally, a very popular newspaper *Davar*, a high-circulation title (the Histadrut office gave the figure of 12,000; the paper's office: 9,000). One way or another, the Histadrut controls a long list of organizations and institutions. With its network of branches, an efficient bureaucratic apparatus, and large financial resources, the Histadrut is indeed a power in the land. Private colonists have to reckon with it and it makes their business that much more difficult. It regulates the flow of the workers to settlements and organizes strikes with precision and ruthlessness, which is always based on a sure-fire calculation. These people do not just call strike on a "Let's just see!" or "We'll show you!" whim, which could easily end in defeat. We think of "strike" as something like a battle, a revolutionary act, even heroic. But for them it is a purely practical, technical measure, quite prosaic. Today, when one of the crises we are going through is that of socialism (and at this juncture I am not going into whether it's transitory or brought about by what causes; I only have in mind facts such as rise of fascism, the inexplicable feebleness of German social democracy under Hitler, the current state of Austria and Poland, MacDonald's "betrayal,"[2] and the fall of Australian government),[3] perhaps the power of Palestinian socialism, too, is

---

2   Ramsey MacDonald's resignation and collapse of the British Labour government in 1931.
3   Fall of the Australian Labor government in 1932. (Transl.)

declining from its zenith. But even those who would agree with this assessment cannot deny that the Histadrut has achieved its influential position thanks to a skillful politics of small steps and is now making good use of it in the interest of the Palestinian proletariat. One may not believe in its formula for solving the Arab question, but one must admit it is a solution which they implement with great style—which means that the party has taken upon itself not just a class problem, but also a weighty national one. Last but not least, by maintaining a good relationship with the private colonists, the party has shown that understands and appreciates the benefits the country accrues from its rich agriculture. Palestinian socialism is a hundred percent socialism: it introduces big reforms, it builds the whole country in the full sense of the word, and it is also radical in its drive to set up agricultural communes. And yet. . . . And yet, if it came to saving our own agriculture I would pray for a government inspired by Palestinian socialism.

The coat of arms of the sport club features a hammer and a sickle. These are not the accessories of any sporting activity I know of. Hammer and sickle—that looks like a Soviet fashion statement, to put it mildly. One of the Histadrut's buildings in Tel Aviv is called the Red House; that's not quite "mainstream" either. Socialist sportsmen do not play against the Maccabi, because the Maccabi is a bourgeois club and the proletariat must not have any contact with the bourgeoisie. The agricultural communes, widely known under their Hebrew name as *kibbutzim* or *kvutzot*, are called "collectives" by our Russian-speaking lecturer. He stresses that children, from the day they are born, are taken away from their mothers and transferred to a separate house, for child rearing is also "collective," and that they belong to the collective, not to a family. He stresses—looking at me sternly with that same "collective" power of expression like a priest expounding a religious dogma—that in *kibbutzim* everything is communal, including clothes. Including clothes . . .

Socialism . . .

***

We are in a different room now, but here too the Russian language resounds. Again—fast, crisp, and hard. And again, it somehow does not fit into the hot softness of the subtropical garden seen through the window. . . .

For the 45,000 Palestinian workers, for the Arab workers who join the Histadrut, for the future masses of the Jewish workers whom the British will allow, eventually, into Eretz Israel, the Histadrut Haovdim puts roofs over their heads, builds socialist proletarian districts, estates, houses. . . .

And so:

"Up until 1931, we have built homes for 3,000 families. . . . "

I am writing this all down, hunched over my notebook, quickly, in short-hand, without thinking, when a word stops me dead in my tracks:

"Families?!"

"Da, familii," the lecturer replies to me. "Familii."

He is surprised by my question. Have I misheard? No, I heard it right. Why did a simple, ordinary word like "family" jar, as if in the flow of that Soviet jargon I misheard it, misunderstood it?

Then I hear again:

"In the single year of 1931 alone, we built houses for 7,000 families. All on Keren Kayemet land."

No, that's funny, the word jarred again. And even the lecturer pronounced it somehow differently, as if hesitating.

" . . . We are building three types of accommodation. One: apartment blocks—120 apartments, most with a kitchen, two rooms, a bathroom, bal-cony. Bigger apartments too. All cooperatives.

"Two: not centrally, but in the suburbs—small, self-contained houses, each with a small garden, 400 square meters each.

"Three: outside towns, at least 3 km—small, self-contained family houses, but with bigger gardens, 1,000–2,000 square meters.

"Four: house collectives—each family in one room, children housed sepa-rately, away from parents, communal kitchen, communal clothes. . . . "

Here our lecturer stops. I'm in with a question:

"What type of accommodation do you build most often?"

The answer is short: the least common is type four. In fact there is only one like that, in Ramat Rachel, built for eighty families. In Haifa, there is to be one for 150 families. The most often built types are two and three. A whole district in Tel Aviv, a housing estate in Jerusalem, another in Haifa—all are like that. In Shekhunat Borokhov, there are already 200 families with another 140 to be settled soon. In Haifa, there are already 180, with building in progress for 200 more. . . . "

Ah, so that's how it is.

And in that moment, with the "Ah, so that's how it is" everything turns around. If before I was bombarded with all that jargon and Soviet phraseology, now the attack falters and folds. I move on to a counterattack. It is well camou-flaged by questions, reflections, and general curiosity.

"So, gentlemen, you say that out of the four types of workers' accommodation built by the Histadrut, the least common is type four?"

No, I'm not mistaken. My "Red" interlocutor takes the question as an attack. But now his swagger is gone, and with it that direct, lofty delivery.

"Yes, it is."

"So"—and I stress that "so"—"the most common types built by you"—and I stress that "you"—"are types two and three?"

"Yes, they are."

These answers sound weak. The man who a moment ago was bombarding me with an armful of arguments is now empty-handed. He is not wasting his forces on more sorties and denials.

I'm going in with a dagger.

"If I understood correctly all the information presented here, the least popular are type four communal houses. This repudiates the idea that families want communal dwellings, since they are collective dwellings where children, clothes, and food are held in common and where each family has the right only to its own separate room. Types two and three, on the other hand, are individual family dwellings, separate units with gardens, which are privately owned. Something like workers' villas."

One has to be familiar with the Marxist atmosphere prevalent in the room to understand how provocative, and funny, it is to join these two innocent words together: "workers" and "villas."

But even now my interlocutor cannot deny what I have pointed out. He can't, can he?

So, on with a final assault:

"The Histadrut Haovdim, the workers organization, is building a new socialist system in Palestine. True? Building house collectives is, of course, cheaper than building whole new estates of family homes. A house collective, as I understand socialism, is a more progressive form, better attuned to a future collective system than privately owned individual houses, that well-known dream of all clerks and teachers. You, gentlemen, a powerful socialist union, instead of leading the masses to socialism, help them to the ideal of small-time capitalism. Thus, gentleman, you are forming a petite bourgeoisie out of those masses that you have the means to lead whatever you like—a class scorned by Marxists."

The argument hits the gentleman from the Histadrut hard, very hard. One has to be a socialist to understand how hard. Indeed—a socialist organization, one of the most powerful in the world, working to transform the proletariat into a petite bourgeoisie . . . ! Why then all this pretense, the comedy about the Hapoel football team refusing to play with the Maccabi because they are bourgeois while Hapoel is proletarian and any contact between them would be a betrayal of one's own class, an obliteration of the eternal—and essential—dogmatic differences between one and the other? Why? If in an area a thousand times more important than a football pitch the proletariat is given the same life goals as the bourgeoisie, even offered private ownership instead of being told to take it from others, when it is simply brought level with a clerk, a village doctor, a shop assistant or a trader—why? And to think that all this is the work and policy of none other than a socialist trade union!

So, gentlemen . . . ?

That was the last question I was going to ask. The last shot in the battle that was conducted by way of questions, never assuming the form of a direct attack. I didn't quite expect to hear a serious counterargument. What I did expect was some kind of an excuse. For instance, that building one big house is not really cheaper than building several dozens of small individual houses. Or that the proletarian homeowner does not necessarily abandon his Marxist ideals; that it does not mean selling out to the petite bourgeoisie. Yes, that is what I expected—excuses, muddying the waters, and ducking responsibility for betraying the doctrine one so publicly avows. The man before me no longer talks fast, trying to pack into his short presentation a whole arsenal of arguments. He no longer sits before me holding forth, the man who so obviously enjoyed crushing his nonsocialist audience with the weight and siren beauty of Soviet terminology. But there is something in the vulnerability of a man scrambling disarmed out of his deep trench that makes my ironic smile fade on my lips.

The man says:

"Sir, our workers want to live like that. We think they are mistaken. We think that those ideals are contrary to socialism. But we have come to the conclusion that making the proletariat happy is more important than building socialism. And happiness is subjective. So we are building these, in your words, 'workers' villas.' . . . "

From the mouth which pronounced the word "collective" the way a prisoner says "freedom," the word "villa" sounds flat. For an idealistic socialist to admit that the workers dream of bourgeois happiness, and more—that a socialist organization is helping them make that dream come true—is nothing short of capitulation. And it is. I can see the man feels it. Thinking: damn, we are beaten.

But I do not think like that. Not at all. For the first time in my talks with the Histadrut I feel truly defeated. Defeated as a man who as a journalist can treat socialism objectively, but as someone who also, though not a "capitalist," feels repelled by Soviet-style collectivization, someone who has seen more of Soviet Russia than many others have read about. I am convinced my interlocutor does not even suspect it.

We get up. Before taking my leave I say:

"Thank you very much. What I've heard and seen here is truly impressive. I have some sympathy for socialism, but also many reservations. So take my good impression that much more seriously."

The socialist looks hesitant.

"And do you know why? Not only because without any supportive legislation which other countries may have, without the help of a left-wing government, you have achieved so much. It is because, as a nonsocialist, I have to admit that you bring real happiness to the proletarian masses. Real happiness against all odds. If need be—even against your own doctrine."

10

Like Stones Thrown against a Bulwark

A dusty Palestinian bus disgorged us at a chaotic assemblage of huts and houses, in the middle of what could be called a steppe if it weren't for two lines of hills fencing it on both sides. The "town" is reminiscent of one of those horse-changing outposts from the era of the stage coach. Nevertheless it is a town; it will be the third new town in Palestine. For Afula sits at a junction of roads from Tel Aviv to Haifa and from Haifa to the Jordan valley; or, to be precise, the Rutenberg's electric power station. And last but not least, Afula lies right in the middle of Emek Israel. The Valley of Jezreel, a wide plain falling away from Haifa towards Jordan, hosts scores of big agricultural settlements but has no "town." Afula will grow here just like Tel Aviv has grown out of the *pardes* colonies surrounding it.

But this is in the future, and before it comes we are walking along the road across fields, which do not grow oranges as in the Jaffa groves, but green and short—shorter than our Polish ones—cereal crops. The sight makes my companion happy, the way vineyards would make us happy in Poland, just as people here are happy seeing each newly built house, each new tree planted, where swamps once used to be, with every mile of new road open to traffic. If back there, near Jaffa, was Palestine's treasury, here it is her breadbasket. My companion Leib Buchner is a young Polish Jew who worked as a teacher in Różan and is now a member of the radical socialist party the Hashomer Hatzair and for the last few months a kibbutznik near Hadera. This is his first time in Emek. We set off together on this trek across the land of cooperatives, aiming to make our way all the way to Jordan and reach the oldest of Jewish agricultural collectives in Tiberias. And to see and learn.

It must have been four o'clock in the afternoon when we walked into the large courtyard of the kibbutz Merhavia. Most of the kibbutzniks were out in the fields. The courtyard's square was closed on three sides with buildings. Before us stood three houses with pretty green shutters and yellow walls. On the left, some old, somewhat rundown farm buildings. Behind us, a third row of buildings housed the kitchens, pantry, a big dining hall, and bathrooms. From where we stood, it all looked like a typical Polish manor. Only the huge tower in the middle, resting on four concrete pillars, bearing a water tank, looked out of place, even exotic.

Soon, a young worker greeted us and Buchner asked for Meir Ya'ari.[1] Ya'ari, as I'd already learned, was the pride of Merhavia. Merhavia belongs to several *kibbutzim* that are governed by—or, I should say, within the sphere of influence of—the Hashomer Hatzair. Ya'ari is one of its leaders and he lives here. He is not back from work yet; this week, it's his turn with the horses and he won't return from the field till later. But the young kibbutznik is free and he is showing us around. First we see a large modern cowshed with concrete troughs. The cows are a local breed, a cross of Damascene and Dutch. Forty-five of them in Merhavia give 500 liters of milk a day, most of which is then turned into cheese and butter. The milk produced by several hundred sheep is also processed here. The diary and cheese shops do not look particularly modern, but they are very clean and their cleanliness does not feel just for show.

Next we visit the henhouse and the incubators. These are set out—to my layman's eye—in an exemplary way. A few more are being built. Soon they will have 1,300 hens and chickens. The young kibbutznik and Buchner explain to me that the dairy and poultry are the most profitable production lines here. As new towns and cities around them grow, the farm can count on steady demand.

Having seen the farmyard, we are just getting to the living quarters when we bump into Meir. He has just had a wash and changed from his work clothes, as all the kibbutzniks do after returning from the field. He is a stocky, strongly built man, older than other workers already seen during our tour of Merhavia, who were mostly in their twenties. He reminds me of those Silesian worker activists, and one from a factory rather than a member of the intelligentsia. I am interested in this man, curious about what he has to say, this socialist-cum-stable boy, member of the Jewish Palestinian "parliament." I have heard a lot about

---

1   Meir Ya'ari—(1897–1987), born in Kończuga, Galicia, in the Austro-Hungarian Empire; an Israeli politician, educator, and social activist in Mandate Palestine and the State of Israel; leader of Hashomer Hatzair, the Kibbutz Artzi movement, and Mapam Party member of the Knesset. (Transl.)

him, and here he is, living on a kibbutz and driving horses. When he opens his mouth it is only to inform me that out of 2625 dunams 2200 are arable land, eighty make up a young *pardes*, and another eighty are the location of an equally young vineyard, orchard, and a vegetable patch.

We come to the water tower standing in the middle of the courtyard. Meir begins to explain how the water has to be drawn from remote wells, how it serves as a local well, and how the lack of water for irrigation is nevertheless a constant problem. Then he moves on to tell us how he arrived here, nearly eight years before, all the way from Rzeszów, with the idea for this kibbutz. How they worked building roads, towns and in the fields for private colonists. He tells us also how the old cooperative of Merhavia began to falter and how they were then leased a colony, together with the buildings, some stock, and inventory; whatever else they needed they bought. Meir shows the tractors, a gift from Keren Hayesod, and a huge "combine," an American harvester which cost $1,800; two years later, two-thirds of the sum has been recouped. It is a fantastic machine, rarely seen on younger and less affluent *kibbutzim*. Merhavia had spare cash as it saved on outbuildings and houses. A Keren Hayesod investment came to £7,362 sterling, which translates into 800 Polish zlotys of inventory per hectare.

On these 260 hectares there live fifty-six grownups and a dozen or so children. We are inside one of the homes. Bright nurseries, white beds, children's furniture. In each room a mother is tucking in her child. The work is over and parents come to see their children. I am struck again by these kids: almost all are flaxen-haired blond with cornflower-blue, Slavic eyes. They could easily be taken for Germans, from Mecklenburg or East Prussia. A weird transformation. At the same time, observing the parents I notice that they, too, look somehow different from the usual physical Jewish type of the Diaspora. Perhaps it is the effect of the sun, manual work, a different climate? Whatever it is, these people have changed since they left their native Tarnóws, Rzeszóws, or Jasłos.[2]

The rooms are a good size, now flooded with setting sun. They are very clean and cozy. Flowers on windowsills, next to beds, sofas with piles of embroidered cushions. Photographs. Mostly of children. One single room is a family home. Each family (and here "family" means a married couple) has a room like this. The "free ones" (and these are rare here) live two or three to a room.

---

2   Tarnów, Rzeszów, Jasło—towns in southeastern Poland, before World War II in what was central Galicia. (Transl.)

Outside on a bench, on the corner of the last house, there sits an old Jew. He speaks Polish better than I speak Hebrew. Buchner explains: in many well-settled *kibbutzim* some people bring over their old parents. They live there supported by the community. He is one of such people. We go into his room. An old Jewish woman asks us about Tłumacz and Trembowla; like many in Merhavia, she too is from Galicia. In the elderly couple's room, whose children returned to the Promised Land, there stands a seven-armed metal Menorah.

It is dark by the time we walk into the dining room and sit on a long wall bench behind the table. A sweet fish dish is served, as well as hot comforting soup and a roast with lots of vegetables and olives. We sit surrounded by the kibbutzniks. And again I am struck how young they all look. Very few seem definitely over thirty. Except for Ya'ari. But at the same time even the youngest ones do not look like what colloquially might be called—unkindly, but accurately—intellectuals. It being a Sabbath evening, all are dressed up in fresh, clean clothes from the common wardrobe.

After dinner, tea is served and the meal is transformed into a "meeting." In view of tomorrow's holiday, the kibbutzniks will have a discussion. Tonight's subject is, I'm told, revisionism. Revisionism, or Jewish fascism—as the invaluable young Buchner explains to me—has grown in the Diaspora lately, and it looks like it may spread in Palestine too. I understand it is a matter of great importance in this kibbutz, where the socialist Hashomer Hatzair rules. The speaker is Praji.[3] He too is one of the elders, though completely different from Meir Ya'ari. He has a Ya'ari head, a typical dogmatist, someone for whom polemic is his natural element, a battle of ideas. And it shows. Praji is holding forth, while my neighbors on the right and on the left help with short summaries of the speech. Young Buchner is resting his head and listening attentively; he will give me his précis later.

At first, the most frequent words I hear are "fascism," "Mussolini," or "Hitler," but then *Polanya* crops up too. Thanks to my neighbors, I can follow the speech in Hebrew. And it goes something like this: the crisis has stirred up reactionary, fascist, tendencies across the world. Each kind of fascism, argues Praji, is closely linked to antisemitism. But then the speaker comes around to a tough nut to crack—what about Italy? He says Italy is an exception, that the good relationship between Jews and Mussolini is the result of the fact that

---

3   Praji—possibly Eliezer Peri (1902–1970), born Eliezer Wileder-Frei in Suchorów, Galicia, in the Austro-Hungarian Empire; Israeli politician, one of the founders of the Kibbutz Artzi movement and of the kibbutz Merhavia; probably the author's mispronunciation of the name. (Transl.)

before the advent of fascism the situation in Italy was less strained than in other places, not as complicated as in Germany. Poland, for Praji, proves a difficult one too. There, he claims, the opposition are antisemitic, not fascist. On the other hand, in fascist Germany, the theory of Zionist socialism reigns unchallenged. Only after this preamble does he deal with revisionism, claiming it is "Jewish fascism." Was the preamble intended to advance the idea that since all fascism is antisemitic, then Jewish fascism is too . . . ? The concept of revisionism itself is given a rather superficial overview.

The discussion is opened by a young man, who has been taking copious notes and now addresses all the points. Basically, his position is not much different from Praji's, perhaps more optimistic if anything. He thinks that all fascisms have very short lives before them. He also claims that if Polish fascism has not gone "for antisemitism," it is only because Poland is not an industrialized country and is therefore experiencing a lesser crisis, and also that Polish fascism was introduced by people who supported it "against themselves." Another speaker more or less repeats the arguments, while another wants to draw attention to the ever-growing danger of revisionism.

I am more interested in the kibbutzniks' *attitude* towards this typically "internal" Jewish discussion than the content itself, which, despite the repeated emphasis by all the speakers that the danger of fascism is now at the country's gates, was difficult to fathom. Few people take part in the discussion. Even fewer listen to it, it seems. Girls and boys keep sneaking out one after another into the courtyard, by now covered in darkness, others just nod off.

When towards the end of the discussion Ya'ari takes the floor, people wake up. Clearly he has this effect on them. He speaks very slowly, as if thinking on his feet; the summary of his speech given to me is rather perfunctory. It seems his appraisal of the argument for the short life of fascism is rather skeptical. As he points out, it was German workers who voted for Hitler. He also points out that fascism has a program of social reforms and that it is implementing it, after its own fashion. He points out its growing strength. And he quotes Turgenev and Tolstoy, though I cannot from what texts.

One cannot say the Merhavia kibbutzniks are indifferent to this weighty problem. They are simply tired. For most part, they agree with the line of argument presented by Praji and others. They accept the words, like the flock accepts the words of truth given to them from the pulpit. Praji, to some extent, meets the kibbutz's ideological needs. He delivered a long, solid, well-argued socialist sermon, out of which his flock distilled the most indispensable elements.

* * *

Bedtime was a relief for all of us. I was put up near the children's home, in a room shared with two others. We crossed the big courtyard. It was on the upland rising above the wide valley of Emek. Its fields were swathed in mist, not so long ago malarial, and the moist warmth of the Levantine night. Far ahead of us to the east spreads the low country, the land of cooperative Emek.

And then, just as at Petah Tikva, in the midst of the quiet Palestinian night, I was told one of those stories of conquest. It went like this:

Palestine's largest valley, once a flourishing land, under the Ottomans turned into a huge swamp. The swamp stretched all the way to Nahalal, almost to the Haifa bay. From the hills of Galilee the colonist *halutzim* looked down into the great valley which the Bible described as the land of milk and honey of their forefathers. The marshes were heated by the subtropical sun, drawing from them the mist of unhealthy effluvia. The deep swamps swallowed people just like those of Pińsk[4] and their malarial air poisoned even neighboring lands. And all was empty.

But the Jews wanted to live there, in the biggest valley in their rocky fatherland. Many times it was judged impossible. At long last, after the Great War, Keren Kayemeth appointed three committees of specialists and sent them to assess once and for all if the land could be colonized, at least by cooperatives of workers. All three committees reported to Menahem Ussishkin, the head of Keren Kayemeth, that it could not be done: Emek Israel was impossible to drain.

Ussishkin thought long and hard. Never before were the specialists so unanimous. Ussishkin, who had spent his life building new Palestine, was in two minds. Finally, he calls the workers —"Three committees said Emek was uninhabitable," he says, "but it's not the committees who are to colonize it, but you. You form your own committee and see for yourselves."

"I knew one of those workers personally," my companion said. "And this is what he told me:

"We went way past Merhavia and we tramped around all day. Swamps, swamps, swamps. No waterfowl, nothing, deadness. Somewhere near the top of the hills, some Arab mud huts. And we tramped and tramped, none of us saying anything. What we saw was a malarial swamp of death, that's what they

---

4   Pińsk—a historical Polish city, after World War II in USSR, now in Belarus, located at the confluence of the rivers Pina and Pripyat, in the region known as Pińsk Marshes; before World War II, it was host to a significant Jewish population. (Transl.)

called it, for there were no other words to describe it, except those words of despair. So we didn't say anything. . . .

"And so we tramped around it—there was no way to cross it—this Emek of ours. The old Merhavia was the last outpost; from then on just bog. So we went back to town and back to Ussishkin. 'Well?' asks Ussishkin.

"We didn't know what tell him. So we didn't say anything. 'So what are you going to tell your comrades?' asked Ussishkin. So one of us said, Mr. Chairman, sir, what can we tell? When a mother has two children, one healthy, the other lame and in fever, then, Mr. Chairman, sir, which one will she go to first?"

And then my companion told me how an army of the *halutzim* descended on the valley. These were not the individual private colonists of the old times. One after the other, landing on the swamps were troops of young workers. A section of the mire—157,227 dunams—was cut up into ditches.

In the suffocating fumes of the bog, in the heat of the Palestinian summer and in the cold of spring, half-naked *halutzim* stood up to their waists in water and dug ditches. A meter and half deep. They worked with their backs bent for hours on end, dredging the mud and throwing it out of the ditch, pushing the spade deeper and further. Swarms of mosquitos buzzing above their heads. Each day, malaria's invisible hand took someone out, but the gaps were soon filled with the young bodies of new *halutzim* flocking in from the Diaspora, who were picking up the hoe and the spade that slipped from the feverish grip. The gaps were filled so fast that the bog had no time to regain an inch of ground.

During 1922–1923, the lands of Nahalal are malaria-free. In 1922, in the neighborhood of Beth Alef, thirty-three percent workers fall ill; in 1923 only five percent. In the same period in Nahalal the number goes down from ninety to one percent. The work continued in the following years. The *halutzim* live in sheds, the skin on their hands cracked, their feet look like they have been eaten by leprosy. "Truly, everything went differently here from the way it normally does in the world—before they build houses, they built a cemetery. But Emek Israel is flooded by ever-new forces. Today, you walk through blossoming villages that enjoy the fruits of that labor. Beautiful is our Emek."

Trekking across Emek Israel

The next day, we left Merhavia as planned, though not before being shown, by the ever-so-obliging Praji, around Emek's new central hospital, new and clean like most of the buildings in the area. Despite being prepared and wearing the right kind of clothes for walking, the heat soon started bearing down on us. From hill-nestling Merhavia, the road ran down to the bottom of the valley, which once—nine, eleven years ago?—was covered by deepest swamps and where now a system of drains collected water from the fields on both sides. Here and there along the way stood groves of young eucalyptus trees with their narrow slender leaves, so reminiscent of white birch; these trees, natural water pumps, marked the new border of the swamps. Stretching around were fields which looked like normal fields of wheat and barley, sometimes potatoes. And meadows. And heat. We passed a trilingual—English, Arabic, Hebrew—sign informing us we had reached sea level and from now on—further towards Jordan and the Dead Sea—we would be below it. Gesher would be the deepest point, some 200 meters below sea level. Gesher is not a kibbutz, but a *kvutzah*. Buchner explains the difference.

Both kibbutz and *kvutzah* are collectives. A *kvutzah* is a small closed collective; once it is constituted as a company it does not accept any new members. A kibbutz, on the other hand, is an open collective, a bit like a village, and sometimes numbering several hundred people. Of course, there are smaller ones too—like Merhavia, for instance—but they are still open to new members.

Kibbutz and *kvutzah* are founded basically on the same principles, differing only in customs and the needs they are set up to meet. The main difference is that in a kibbutz the highest law and rule is the general assembly of all its members. These will take place relatively often, certainly when an important decision has to be taken. I noticed yesterday in Merhavia how keenly people stressed that there were no "officials" or "authorities" in the kibbutz, just "civil servants." They form a collegial body of administration, which is then split into different functions. And so the chief figures are the "general manager," who oversees the kibbutz's economy; the "secretary," whose job it is to maintain contact with the outside world, a kind of kibbutz "minister for foreign affairs"; and the "treasurer," whose function is often reduced to book keeping and, as such, tends to be merged with the function of the general manager. Apart from these, there are two more "functionaries," who set up the timetable for different jobs and appoint people to do them. Quite outside this system is the position of "elder"—directly responsible to state authorities.

As we walk along the sandy field road, my conversation with Buchner blends in my mind with the talk I had yesterday with the kibbutzniks. The interrelations between *kibbutzim* vary. There is a theory according to which a kibbutz is independent of others, and certainly is not part of a hierarchy. But then, according to another theory, a kibbutz is only one cell of a bigger, national collective. Generally, the newer *kibbutzim* are closely connected to each other. And all, one way or the other, are affiliated with a particular political party. Thus, Buchner tells me, there are five to seven *kibbutzim* connected with the Hashomer Hatzair. Together they form an arch-kibbutz, a national one, with a council and executive comprised of seven members. These are so-called *shomrov kibbutzim* ("guardian," derived from the name of the Hashomer Hatzair)—guardians of the reclaimed land, of course.

The vast majority of the *kibbutzim*, however, are under the influence of the Palestine's Workers Party (a socialist party that belongs to the Second International) which rules within the Histadrut Haovdim. These are the *halutzim kibbutzim*. They are even more closely interconnected than the shomrov and are united as the Kibbutz Hameuhad—the United Kibbutz Movement. Whereas at a *shomrov*, a kibbutznik is a member of just one kibbutz and only as a consequence a member of the union of *kibbutzim*, with the Kibbutz Hameuhad the procedure is the other way round. First, one becomes a member of the general organization and only then is allocated to a particular kibbutz, the allocation decided according to local needs and requirements. As for the *kvutzot*, even they have started working towards tighter integration and have formed a federation—Hevra Hakvutzot. All of these supra-collectives are first and foremost seen as mutual help organizations for all individual settlements.

It being Sabbath, and a hot one, the fields are practically empty. By midday, having passed several less interesting *kibbutzim*, we arrive at Kfar Yehezkel, a lovely, sprawling settlement, whose red-roofed small houses are engulfed, just like those near Tel Aviv, in the green of the orange groves.

Kfar Yehezkel is a *moshav*, a different kind of agricultural settlement. A *moshav ovdim*—"a working settlement"—is a hybrid private and collective enterprise. Those who lack capital or whose principles prevent them from setting up a private cooperative, such as the people at Petah Tikva, settle in a *moshav ovdim*.

A *moshav* functions along the following rule: each settler is the owner of a plot of land leased to him by Keren Kayemet—he cannot sell it for any other price than the one he originally paid for it, nor to anyone not accepted by Keren Kayemet; he cannot use hired labor either; all field work—ploughing, sowing, harvesting—is equally shared, and all things related to it are decided by the *moshav*'s management, which is elected from the general assembly of its members; however, the *pardes*, vineyards, reared cattle, and poultry are privately owned by individuals, who also receive their own individual share of the profits derived from the collective fieldwork.

I'm still turning over the term *moshav* in my mind, trying to memorize it, when we reach the first huts of the settlement and enter one of them. The "hut" has several rooms, spotlessly clean, and we are welcomed by children who, naturally, speak only their native Hebrew. In the living room, I'm struck by the view of a strange piece of furniture, something like a big box. At first, I think it's a kind of piano, but then it turns out to be . . . an incubator. Apparently, hatching eggs is also a profitable *moshav* business. That is confirmed by the young farmer of Arab complexion who comes in, called by the children.

He is from Poland, near Tarnów. He emigrated before 1913, so he switches quickly from Polish into German, strongly laced with Yiddish, but even that is a struggle. At last, my comrade Buchner steps in as translator. However, what the farmer has to say is not particularly interesting. He talks about farming problems—ah, not very big—and he talks about the upcoming harvest, eagerly awaited now in Emek. He has three kids, all playing while we talk. I am struck again, just as I was in Merhavia, by these fair, oddly Slav-looking little heads, and the almost Nordic features of their faces.

And then I'm struck by the thought that both our host and his young wife, who has meanwhile arrived and invites us to stay for lunch, that they too represent a different type than that—still sometimes seen here—of their other Tarnów compatriots. Yet one cannot say they don't look Jewish—they do; they just don't make one think of a Jewish ghetto. Perhaps that is exactly the difference between a strong, confident man and a weak, timorous one. Sometimes, even the arrogant Polish Jews sound a false a note (or so it seems to me), have something artificial, unnatural about them. Not these Hebrew farmers.

The nephew of our host, himself recently arrived from Poland, begins to help the indefatigable Buchner. We learn that our host once worked on a kibbutz, from which he transferred to a *moshav*. Why? He explains that in the kibbutz he simply could not come to terms with the fact that nothing was really his. He just could not accept that were he to leave the kibbutz after twenty years, he would leave it empty-handed. "And to have nothing at the end of your life—that's hard, isn't it."

Comrade Buchner, a true collectivist, squirms on the sofa like a devil sprinkled with holy water. Here our host turns to him—naturally, he does not deny that kibbutz economy is generally of a higher order than that of a *moshav*. He does not deny that at Ein Harod an average kibbutznik without a shirt to his name lives a better, more comfortable life than he, the owner of the eleven-hectare plot of land. And yet, the foremost comfort in life comes from exercising one's own free will, self-determination. That means more than—at least for him—better food, a better house, more than all the comforts enjoyed by the kibbutzniks in more affluent *kibbutzim*.

And his own old kibbutz?—It's no more. Fell apart. First they got rid of the communists. "They wanted to impose the Russian way," he says. Then they split into "left" and "right." Then part of them left altogether; they are now in a kibbutz near Hadera. And on top of that the farm itself was badly run. "You see, a kibbutz works well only when all its workers are driven by the same idea. All of them—by the same idea. Otherwise all goes to seed."

The same nearly happened to Kfar Yehezkel. The *moshav* has been existence for a few years now. Without, or nearly without capital, over 400 people have found here, in this intermediate kind of Jewish settlement, a good roof over their heads.

Is it a "halfway house"? After lunching on tasty country food, when we comes to say our goodbyes, I ask my ex-kibbutznik, what his plans are for the future. It turns out he had a ready answer: he is saving up for his very own *pardes*. When the kids grow up, one will stay in the *moshav*, the others will be given their own—as much as possible—private farms to work on. Will he able to save up enough given the growing price of land? Sure, he will, land is not that expensive. Close to Tel Aviv—yes, it is, but further out, near the border with Jordan. . . ? And by then, perhaps, Transjordan will be available too. . . .

The Transjordan mountains, swathed in beige and blue, draw a hazy line in the evening mist and look like a faraway image of Emek projected onto a screen. They can be seen from everywhere, from all the settlements and all the Kfar Yehezkel ex-kibbutzniks; and all the ex-kibbutzniks in dozens of other *moshavot* watch them intently during their afternoon siestas. Just like our host, they think that perhaps one day, thanks to their hard work on the *moshav*, they too will come to have their own private colony, that they too will finally reach the standard of ownership attained now by the sons of pioneers from Petah Tikva and Rikhon LeZion. The *moshav* is the way to return to individual agriculture. For all of them? Of course not. There are enough people who do not get further than the everyday problems of their *moshav*. There will be ideologues, deep-thinking people, who will move on or return to a kibbutz as a higher or even best way of life and economy. I learn about one such case a few days later from Hayuta Bussel in Degania. But for the rest, and probably most of them, the future they strive for is closer to that of Petah Tikva than Merhavia.

12

Sabras of Ein Harod

Still, I kept thinking to myself, with all their orderly, thrifty, and straightforward beauty, those *kibbutzim* are just plain boring. We were leaving Geva, another neighboring kibbutz we passed through on our quick march. An exemplary poultry farm, but not so successful in cereals, despite the great efforts of its youthful workforce and their children. The country collective resounded with German and Russian and in their village library I could leaf through a few pages of the striking work of Oswald Spengler, full of foreboding prophesies.[1] I remembered what Buchner, who met him and discussed the idea of *kibbutzim* with him, told me: "Shame I didn't meet you a week earlier. I would have taken you to our kibbutz in Hadera. We had a great festival, we danced all day. . . ."

"Why?"

"A child was born."

I remembered what Buchner told me because he was just showing me the buildings of Ein Harod: from the slope of the hill run six lines of rooftops belonging to small white house. Below, there is a farm, and above, crowning it all, stand two large modern buildings and between the two, slightly lower, the third, even bigger one. There is a striking contrast between the Corbusier-inspired lines of the multistory structures and the still-wild background of the countryside. The twin buildings are children's homes, where children live "away from families," as they used to say in the Histradut Haovdim. The one between them is the refectory.

---

1   Oswald Spengler (1880–1936)—German historian and philosopher of history, best known for his book *The Decline of the West* (1922), which covered all of world history. Spengler's model of history postulates that any culture is a superorganism with a limited and predictable lifespan. (Transl.)

Merhavia was first a regular settlement and was collectivized later. Ein Harod, before it became a kibbutz, was just a swamp. It is a pure, full-blooded kibbutz. I salute in it the first agricultural collective I have seen in my life, an agrarian settlement of the new type. What will it tell me? What will its people tell me?

To see the kibbutz secretary Yonay we are directed through narrow little streets lined with small bungalows and green, square gardens. I am smiling at my thoughts, which leads Buchner to offer a penny for them.

"You see, this view reminds me of—you know what? Something as old-fashioned as this is modern: a small street that goes past the houses of the Cameldolese Hermite Monastery's monks, in Cracow's Bielany. An old, ascetic Catholic order—and a Jewish collective."

Buchner is not smiling. He says, quite seriously:

"You don't even know how similar they are. . . . "

Yonay looks a typical worker: broad-shouldered, stocky, speaks slowly, thoughtfully. It is his third year here as a kibbutz "functionary." He runs the complex machinery of the collective—which has in its ranks many people with higher-education diplomas—the way one runs a tractor or a tank. He is holding in his hand a Russian worker's cap, the kind Lenin used to clench in a gesture of the people's tribune, seen in old photographs from the time of the revolution. He is show us ploughs and sowing machines, taking us around the cowshed, long like a turbine hall. Then we move onto the living quarters positioned above the farm.

This Cubist-inspired construction, which contains the kitchen and a dining hall, feels like a modern sanatorium. It is perhaps the clean tables and walls, the row of windows looking out on the sunny slopes of the Mount Gilboa where the first Jewish king fell on his sword, which give that impression. It's teatime, so we sit down at a table. Yonay answers my questions, asked by Buchner.

And so it goes again:

The 80,000 dunams cereal farm, launched five years ago, still brings no profit. The kibbutz relies on poultry, sold mostly to Tel Aviv. And it looks healthy for it. The annual tax burden is the £250 sterling for the land and £50 for the buildings. Of the latter they have over forty. As a cereal farm it is also taxed and the tax is £130 a year.

There are 120 families living in the kibbutz, 180 children, thirty unmarried and fourteen old ones, brought over from the Diaspora. The old folks have a kosher kitchen, and they've even built a synagogue for them. . . .

Here I interrupt:

"And you—don't you go to synagogue?"

Buchner, answering for himself, reminds me he's already said that the kibbutzniks are atheists. But Yonay cuts in with the remnants of his Russian:

"There are a few that do go, two or three. . . . "

"And you," I ask him, "are you religious?"

Yonay smiles broadly, but it is a different kind of a smile from the one with which the *halutz* watched the praying Jew on the *Dacia*. He answers in Hebrew—no. "Not now. But, when I get old, who knows. . . . "

✳ ✳ ✳

I met a young teacher from Poland who had been living in the kibbutz with her daughter for over a year now. She showed me all the modern conveniences in the two childrens' homes. I'm not sure if I would feel comfortable there myself: it looks like a hospital and nursery rolled into one. But apparently the children playing there felt good enough. There was only a handful of them. We watched the farm below, from the balcony, as the horses which had just been unharnessed from the ploughs were mounted by the youngest kibbutz offspring learning to horse ride with the help of their parents. Here, as in Merhavia yesterday, after the field work was done, all the children played together with their parents.

Buchner, ever the pedagogue, approached some of them and in a moment we were surrounded by a bunch of kids. They gave off an odd kind of fearless openness. They were surprised when they learned we weren't staying for good. For if not, why did we come?

I had a good long chat with them and their teachers. Parents also came up to talk. The teachers, in white coats, and I, a Polish journalist, all stooped over an unruly bunch of little heads, a bunch of little heads all bursting with questions, a gang of kids for whom the best houses were being built and who were to receive the best kibbutz possible. To rear them, to breed them.

These kids were all born in Palestine, not in the Diaspora. For them, the Płoskirów[2] pogrom and recent events are going to be history, just like Kroże[3]

---

2 Płoskirów—a town in Western Ukraine, named Proskurov when part of the Russian Empire; from 1954, named Khmelnitskyi; in 1919, the site of a pogrom (also known as the Proskurov pogrom), which was carried out by the Ukrainian People's Army under General Semysenko. (Transl.)

3 Kroże—a small historic town in today's Lithuania; in 1891, the site of the Kroże massacre, when Russian Cossacks attacked Polish Catholics defending their church against conversion

was for us, and for our children will be Radzymin.[4] These Palestine-born kids are colloquially called "sabras," after the common shrub seen growing everywhere here.

The sabras of Ein Harod, laughing and vivacious, saw us off the following day, waving to us as we were leaving on our next leg of the Emek trek. I thought of the poor noisy, sickly weaklings from our ghettoes. If we were to compare the two, the sons of one and the same nation, put standing side by side and showed to people, perhaps then they could clearly see the difference, the vast distance that lies between the world of the Diaspora and the newly found fatherland.

---

to Orthodox *tserkov'* (faith); the event, publicized in the European press, made Russia ease up on its forceful Russification program. (Transl.)

4   Radzymin—a small town near Warsaw, the place of a major battle on August 15, 1920, when the Polish Army stopped the advance of the Red Army. (Transl.)

13

Gesher

Over the next few days, we passed Tel Josef (which split away from the kibbutz of Ein Harod), the two white blocks of its modern courtyard rising right across from the old kibbutz and Beth Alef with its sprawling low houses huddled under the massif of Mount Gilboa. The lowest point of the Jordan Rift Valley, where the river flows into the Dead Sea, we reached by train. We literally stumbled into it at the end of a hot, muggy evening, accompanied by the faraway drone of the turbines at the Palestinian Dnieprostroi[1]—Rutenberg Power Station. We spent the night at the *kvutzah* Gesher. It's a relatively new settlement, but its housing is still mostly sheds, where one is bothered by mosquitoes and other nocturnal bugs. The apparent poverty amidst these "fat years" has luckily spared one thing—food. There is just about the right number of people here not to go hungry.

Gesher has 1,000 dunams of land, right on the other side of its fence. But Gesher lies outside Emek and its land climbs up the Jordan hills, one of the most arid areas in the world. Out of those 1,000 dunams, only 250 are cultivated, and even that was a great struggle. There is also very little livestock. And so the dairy business, which we saw blooming in other *kibbutzim* of the Emek, is also lacking. The main reason being that, unlike on the rich high pastures of Emek Israel, the conditions for cattle raising here are very difficult. And another is the lack of markets; just a stone's throw away Transjordan begins, but at this point of time it's still a desert.

---

1   Dnieprostroi—the Dnieper Hydroelectric Station in Ukraine, one of the first and largest dams built in the Soviet Union, attaining legendary status as the supreme achievement of the Soviet economy; in 1941, it was destroyed on Stalin's orders, the tidal wave killing thousands of civilians and retreating Red Army troops. (Transl.)

So they turned to another line of business—bananas—and planted fifty dunams in one go. Unfortunately, the crop failure, which has affected the Gesher region three years in a row, did not spare the banana plantation. It was burned by the sun and frozen by the cold. To the Gesher workers who pass the sad withered sticks on their way to work it looks like a cemetery—here lies buried £2,500.

The bananas were the final blow for the *kvutzah*. Its debt amounts to £5,000. This has been growing for years and now they are behind with the repayments for the machinery. The British bailiffs do not come to take their property (such a protective policy towards agriculture is nothing unusual here; even three-year debts are sometimes written off). But the debt still hangs over the *kvutzah*. Disaster. Crisis. A crash.

The people who came to Gesher on the Jordan left their homes in Galicia or Transylvania, had to overcome thousands of obstacles and stood guard for over a thousand and one nights in fear of Bedouin attacks. From the twelve first founders, the *kvutzah* has grown to a bigger than usual size of 140 adults and thirty-two children. They sat down and talked and talked to us. From the Rothschild PICA they received 3,000 dunams. It lay further from the *kvutzah*, but it looked promising. Alas, these hopes also failed. Disputes over the lease, and other political and economic issues with the PICA, dragged on. And the Rothschild land was also hit by crop failure. They tried oranges and vines. The 110 dunams of *pardes* stand out as one source of profit in the otherwise negative Gesher budget, but this plus is very small indeed.

If Gesher survives and still keeps going, it is thanks to the special labor system which has helped many a poorer kibbutz to get back on its feet. Some half a mile and one bridge away there stands the "Rutenberg station"[2] which harvests electric power from the dam on the river Jordan and its tributaries. The construction of the station and its further development required a sizeable workforce. The capitalist neighbor propped up the collectivists. Over five years, the station gave employment to forty to fifty of them, and even now fifteen are still still working there. At the beginning, an unskilled laborer, after a short training period, could earn fifteen zlotys a day, and it's still the going rate. The Gesher kibbutzniks, like many of their other comrades from Haifa, sent part of their collective to work for Rutenberg. The other part carried on building Gesher and the farm. The workers' pay was put into the kitty for the upkeep

---

2   Rutenberg Station—the Rutenberg power plant at Naharayim. (Transl.)

and general expenses of the *kvutzah*. The calculated total contribution from this particular source over the five years came to about £20,000.

The story goes that Gesher was initially constituted by people of the extreme left. The PICA—and I have this information directly from them, so it may be biased—having leased the land, is still fighting with them on the "collectivism" issue—"Set up a *moshav* and we'll come to understanding," they say. But the Gesher *kvutzah* is a well-hewn, tight ship by now. They have been fighting off Arab attacks from Transjordan for too long; for too long they have shared their lives together, here on the Palestinian borderlands, just like on the old Polish eastern outposts warding off the Tartars. And for too long they have cried together over the *kvutzah*'s lamentable budget. They don't want to be a *moshav*; they don't want to break up and lose all that experience and history.

In their collective effort the *kvutzah* is thus showing the Rothschild PICA its teeth. The PICA keeps telling them that with the money they have received—£27,000—any other noncollective settlement would have done much better. Perhaps this is true. But they like it like this. It gives them more satisfaction. And memories of the kind one sometimes gets from the army, the front line, battles. It gives them what a *moshav* wouldn't, because it couldn't.

At the same time, while, in the eyes of the Gesher people, the PICA turned into an enemy, the huge concrete slabs which were rising next door were regarded not as capitalist evil but as their best friend. Rutenberg Station, the biggest capitalist industrial colossus in Palestine versus a poor collective of leftists.

14

Glass Towers Are not a Myth[1]

P alestine can feed and maintain a bigger population only as an industrial and urbanized country. The tradition of Tyre and Jerusalem predestined it, as it were, to be the industrial and trading center of the Middle East. It looks like the flow of capital put in motion by Jewish colonization created just such possibilities. But Palestine lacks one indispensable factor for the development of industry—coal. The plan for population growth, being one of the national imperatives, broke down because of the limited possibilities for industrialization due to the shortage of fuel for future factories.

The first big industrial company in the country without coal was the Palestine Electric Company Ltd., founded with the aim of providing a general supply of electric light and power. The genesis of this enterprise was simple, though again, it is one of those founding myths interwoven into the history of Palestine, which could be called the legend of Good Capitalism. It all happened not so long ago, and it went like this:

In one of the big Russian factories, a young engineer called Pinhas Rutenberg,[2] a Jew born into a family swept into the wide river of Russian life,

---

1   Glass houses—a metaphorical image for the rise of modern Poland, which in 1918 regained independence after more than 120 years of partitions; originally used in Stefan Żeromski's novel *Przedwiośnie* (The Coming Spring [Warszawa: Wydawnistwo J. Mortkowicza, 1925]) before entering the colloquial mainstream use as a mythical promise of a bright future that never arrived. (Transl.)

2   Pinhas Rutenberg (1879–1942)—a Russian Jewish engineer, businessman, and political activist; he played an active role in two Russian revolutions, one of the founders of the Jewish Legion and the American Jewish Congress; founded the Palestine Electric Company, currently the Israel Electric Corporation. (Transl.) Before Pinhas Rutenberg became a Zionist, he was a Russian revolutionary of extreme views; apparently, in 1905, in a Finnish villa, he carried out the assassination of an agent provocateur—the famous Gapon. (Author)

was bitten by the bug of Zionism. He carried on as a Russian electrical techni-
cian, continued to study and built up his theoretical and professional knowledge. Like many other ambitious engineers, he dreamed about the new marvels
of technology, the Americanization of Russia, Asia, and the world. He had great
plans, underpinned by his Jewish sense and aptitude for commerce. But one
day, into those plans and sophisticated calculations sneaked another factor,
which played the role of a turning point and refocused the plans of the young
engineer. The new direction shot past the green Russian borders and stretched
down the globe to a small country in the south, where another bunch of poor
dreamers kept sheep and dreamed about vineyards and haymaking.

The first years after the war found Rutenberg in Palestine. In Palestine,
there were many *halutzim* draining marshes and colonists planting oranges and
vine. But not one visionary engineer with technical vision and business acumen
in the grand American style. Hailing from Russia, Pinhas Rutenberg was the
first. He crossed the length and breadth of the Jordan Valley and examined all
its paths and rifts. He then made the usual long and arduous pilgrimage of an
innovator to Palestine's Jewish and British high officials. He went to London
and even further. Everywhere, he was met with polite skepticism and barely
masked suspicion. Everywhere, he unfurled the broad pages of his plans and
drawings on which the blue ribbon of Jordan was cut up by dashes marking
nonexistent dams. He kept repeating his pitch like a prerecorded weather fore-
cast for mushroom picking. For the duration of construction, one river has to
be diverted out of its bed; then this bed fused with the flow of another river to
form a big lake closed off by a dam; which dam should provide a sufficiently
big drop for the falling water to turn four gigantic turbines and thus illuminate
the biblical land. And if that didn't sound convincing enough he added that the
place was extremely remote and located in an of arid desert. It that still did not
convince his listeners he explained that this would be only the first dam. The
ultimate goal was to build eight!

Pinhas Rutenberg's memoirs would make fascinating reading, especially
his door-to-door search for capital. After 1918, Jewish big capital flowed like
a great, wide river into Germany—that young, healthy new democracy. . . .
At the time, the "Palestine" in its ledgers was located along with items such
as "Community Poor," "Father's Memorial Fund," and "Stipends for Sons
of Factory Workers." The engineer who was offering a share in the Palestine
Electric Company Ltd. was shown in reply the receipts for donations to Keren
Hayesod, the Hebrew University, and other charitable foundations in Palestine.

"We have already done our patriotic duty, Mr. Rutenberg. And how are you faring down there in Palestine—alright?"

The stories that circulate in Palestine about those days would make some of those financiers blush and lead them to make a mental note that there was a fantastic investment opportunity which they missed. Nevertheless, the capital was raised and the Palestine Electric Company was founded with Anglo-Jewish capital of £1,000,000. Keren Kayemet and the Jewish National Fund contributed £100,000.

Construction lasted for five years. The great dam which rose in today's Tel Or, holding the waters of the Jordan and Yarmuk in a huge lake more than a dozen meters deep, now stands ready. The area of construction was covered by a town of rooftops and factories. It is cordoned off by a fence of barbed wire, like a camp: not everyone is let in, and only on certain days, and they are not allowed to see everything. The security of this great industrial complex is important not just to the owners, but to the government too. Tourists are normally shown only the great big concrete wall, the dam. Under the roof of a very large hall housing engines and batteries, there are two massive pipes several meters high—the power-producing turbines. Next to them, there is room for two more which will be built later. One day, they will work together, one after the other. One day, at other bends in the river now covered by willow shrubs, there will stand new dams of the Palestine Electric Company Ltd.

But even what stands today is very impressive. The whole country gets its light from here. Other large power-transmission plants, offshoots of Rutenberg's, already exist in Tiberias, Tel Aviv, and Haifa. The dam on the reservoir can produce 400,000 kilowatts. It can illuminate the whole country. But to illuminate is not enough.

Most of the colonies still rely on oil for light. To replace it with electricity is not Rutenberg's chief ambition. This ambition has grown into a big plan, of which Palestine Electric Company speaks very little but which everyone is aware of: to provide Palestine industry, today's and tomorrow's, with cheap power. All the factories and workshops in Palestine—electrification of the whole country!

This plan is already being carried out. According to the latest statistics, which date from 1931, in Tel Aviv alone there are 1400 working electric power plants. In Haifa the number is 650, and in Tiberias, twenty. These numbers will continue to rise together with the living standards of these cities and their populations and the development of industry. The affordability of electric power and the high prices of coal will force all new industries in the world to rely on electricity.

Still, Palestine has another ambition. Its future requires yet another plan to be implemented and calls for new works after the great deeds of Pinhas Rutenberg. It too is almost utopian. But those who have seen the new Palestine will know that this plan is more realistic than some of our simpler ones.

At the moment, on the orange plantations, there are several hundred steam engines pumping water used for irrigation from deep, artesian wells. Orange trees need a lot of water. Oranges are a good crop in Palestine thanks to sufficient irrigation. But cereal crops are in deficit, mostly because their irrigation is insufficient. And it is insufficient because, while the high price commanded by oranges makes irrigation cost-effective, the price of cereals (a hundredweight of wheat retails for around twenty-eight zlotys) makes the irrigation of a field of wheat utterly unprofitable. The main reason for the shortage of cereal crops in Palestine is, then, the lack of a viable irrigation system. This can be remedied in two ways. The first would be an artificial increase in the price of cereals, which would make irrigation possible. The other—the lowering of the cost of irrigation.

Palestine is too sensible to go for the first solution (if it is possible). The second solution is Rutenberg's other plan. This is the final part of his grand design, which officially is still not up for public discussion. To us it sounds crazy to irrigate the land to grow wheat, and with electric power at that. But in Palestine it's no greater a folly than draining the swamps of Emek. More— Emek could be put to more use than it is now. There are large parts of it that require continuous irrigation. Rutenberg, Rutenberg!

That cry—it's a call from the land of collectives, a plea from people who want to see the completion of their lives' work. Rutenberg's station at Tel Or, the Hill of Light, on the map of Palestine looks as if it were the farthest outpost of Emek. It stands, as if showing future colonists the way to the land beyond Jordan. Rutenberg's station is expected to be the first stage of this process: the development of electric power on such a scale the price of electricity will drop so low that it will be commercially viable not only to irrigate orange plantations, but also other, more mundane, crops of the Emek.

And then . . .

* * *

I often asked people, from different walks of life in Palestine, who they thought was the most popular person. The answers were different, but the name of Pinhas Rutenberg was mentioned many times. Interestingly, he turned out to be very popular in Emek. The Red Emek of the collectivists. For people in Tel Aviv, Rutenberg must have been someone like Poznański for Łódź[3]—a great industrialist, with a great head for business and . . . that's all. For the people of Emek, that same man was seen as the successor of the first *halutzim*, who himself has done many great deeds. Rutenberg was seen as a leader and a symbol. Most certainly a symbol, for the interests of the Palestine Electric Company and Palestine itself are one. To a great extent, this is because the man is a true idealist, undeniably: his concern for the workers, his philanthropy, and personal modesty. When I say this, I feel that Pinhas Rutenberg's story may sound like a version of Montesquieu's *Lettres Persanes*, though in a different register; that perhaps this Palestine of mine may be seen by readers as a kind of Atlantis, a mythical place, which I want to present it as a utopian land of harmony between proletarian and capitalist, just like in that popular film *Metropolis*. And yet, that's how it feels. I myself don't know whether I should be pleased with it or disappointed. I'm just noting down my thoughts.

And it's not so utopian as it seems. Rutenberg saved many a sinking *kvutzah* like Gesher and helped many poor people. In Poland, we have a beautiful legend about Queen Kinga, who miraculously transported salt mines from Hungary to Polish Wieliczka.[4] Rutenberg didn't miraculously transport any rich mines from Russia, but instead of black coal he gave Palestine what is colloquially known as "white coal." And how fundamentally different are the farmers from around Wieliczka and the *halutzim* of Emek. The distance between the medieval queen and her dynasty, which apart from herself gave God eleven saints, and a Jewish engineer from Russia, Pinhas Rutenberg, is like a chasm. And yet I feel there is a power on this earth which has built an arch and a bridge over this chasm—the blessing of a good deed.

---

3   Izrael Kalman Poznański (1833–1900)—Polish Jewish businessman, textile magnate, and philanthropist in nineteenth-century Łódź, Poland; one of its three legendary "cotton kings." (Transl.)

4   Wieliczka—a small town in southern Poland, near Cracow, famed for its Wieliczka Salt Mine, one of the world's oldest in continuous operation (from the mid thirteenth century until 2007; in 1978, it was designated a UNESCO World Heritage Site. (Transl.)

In Tel Or, Hill of Light, as Rutenberg named his power station, I talked about Żeromski's *Przedwiośnie*. About the glass houses which old Baryka[5]— who did not make it back to Poland, dying in Russia—kept telling his son he would see when he finally got to Poland, which young Baryka never saw anywhere . . . about how that Polish engineer built a modern power plant utilizing sea currents . . . about the glass houses built in the place of old, smoky cottages . . . about the whole country, warm and brightly lit . . . about a technical vision reaching the heights of myth.

I'm not sure if my readers see in Mr. Rutenberg that old Baryka, but to me the similarities are striking. Tel Or, in view of all that is to come, is but a quarter of the way. But that quarter is already covered. Żeromski's novel is regarded in Poland as a revolutionary work and the author himself as a visionary of revolution. At Tel Or, I was struck by a thought—that Żeromski's ideal is none other than that of an engineer building glass houses, that of a lone genius, not a man of the crowd; that progress is driven by an individual, by his knowledge, not by a party cell. Żeromski's golden dream of a new Poland, his bitter disappointment that such a Poland never emerged—or such a man—was concentrated into Baryka, the great innovator, the great patriot, the great businessman. Businessman? Alright, let's go back to the book, let's see. Żeromski says: *because* there was no such a man in Poland who could build glass houses, *because* there were only vague ideologues, like the good old Gaszyniec[6] with his bleached radicalism in place of a positive program, it was *therefore* natural that the new generation of young Cezary Baryka had no choice but to march on the presidential palace. Because there were many people like Gaszyniec and none like Baryka. No Rutenberg.

This gloss on Żeromski's novel does not quite fit my Palestinian reportage, I'm going right off at a tangent here. But then I don't mean to give any casuist excuses or an apology for capitalism. If the golden dream about a visionary engineer-industrialist, the builder of a better life for the masses, hadn't been dissipated by the parliamentary slothfulness of Gaszyniec and his ilk, today the whole of Poland would be getting high on those popular poster

---

5   [O]ld Baryka—the father of Cezary Baryka, the main character in Żeromski's *The Coming Spring*; he lived and worked in Baku, in imperial Russia, but longed for an independent Poland; after his death, his son Cezary arrived in Poland pursuing his father's dream of return and reconstruction of the old country. (Transl.)

6   Gaszyniec?—probably the author's mistake or a typo for the name Gajowiec. (Transl.)

ads seen at every railway station: "Sugar fortifies!"[7] Still, the point is that even if the glass towers and their builders were in Żeromski's eyes a mere utopia, they were nonetheless an ideal. But the rebellion of the young, the march of the young on the presidential palace guarded by the soldiers, was not just a necessity, but a *sad* necessity, a tragedy. Ah, that myth of glass houses. . . . But Tel Or, Rutenberg—they are not a myth.

---

7   *Cukier krzepi!* (Pol.)—a popular advertising campaign in prewar Poland, promoting the benefits of sugar, devised for the growing sugar industry; the slogan was invented by Melchior Wańkowicz, the editor in chief of the Rój publishing house, another publisher of Pruszyński's *Palestine* (Warszawa: Rój, 1936). (Transl.)

15

From Ghetto to Kibbutz

Palestine has created several dozen collective farms. There are several thousand people living there and several thousand more want to join them. These collectives are prosperous enterprises, even though they are not kept together by force of law or terror, while the capital supported them only reluctantly So, apart from Russia, there is a country whose people have voluntarily abandoned private ownership to the point of forgoing private life, material possessions, even their own clothing. Children are raised whose memory of a different social system will fade, just like the memory of prewar affluence among today's intelligentsia or the memory of serfdom among the peasantry. What we are witnessing here, though on a smaller scale, is an experiment that some people call "the social order of tomorrow," which has so far failed in all its attempts, except those kept alive by force. Some of these "experiments" have been successfully going on for years. Is there a lesson here for us people for whom Palestine is a remote and vague concern? Are we really witnessing the birth of a new social order, a New Man?

* * *

The answer to this question is too important to summarize in a few lines. And it's too difficult to defend against the attacks, which it is bound to provoke from both left and right. Before such an answer can be offered, these are some reflections collected in my notebook over the two weeks' trek around the *kibbutzim*.

16

The Dollar Falls Twenty Percent

I was just leaving Tel Aviv on my way to Emek when the whole bus was suddenly agitated in a way reminiscent of the old Nalewki. A moment later, I learned that it was because of news from the stock exchange—the dollar had fallen by twenty percent!

The fall of the dollar roused emotion that, luckily, did not affect the bus's engine and soon we were in Emek, in Merhavia, which I wrote about earlier. In the evening, when Buchner disappeared somewhere looking for Ya'ari, I sat among the kibbutzniks in the refectory. Someone asked me:

"And what's the news from the world?"

I nearly gave him a quick, perfunctory answer, when I remembered the dollar. My journalistic instinct, of a man whose sole joy is to give people the latest, freshest news, whose greatest days are those with great scoops and evening extras, all of that fused and came out in one sentence:

"Amazing, sensational news—today the dollar fell by twenty percent!"

For a brief moment, there was silence, not followed by any questions. So I pressed on. Having given them the big title, I followed with a sensational dispatch in bold lettering:

"From twenty-seven piastras yesterday, the dollar fell today to twenty-three and its downward slide continues. Which means that the United States are in free fall towards inflation. What president Roosevelt has done is only the beginning, because tomorrow the US Congress will pass new laws that will give him new dictatorial powers over financial policies. The panic will spread to every country that has its reserves in US dollars, founded on the dogma of its indestructibility. . . . "

Nothing. Simply and clearly nothing. No reaction.

At that moment, I was not just surprised—I was given a flick on the nose. All my journalistic pride in knowing exactly what my readers want, my professional confidence in the ability to tell the difference between the sensational and plain boring, all that was smashed against the expectant silence of—"Well . . . ? What else have you got?"

I felt stupid. But at the same time noticed and registered something perhaps more important than the twenty percent fall of the dollar. On the Merhavia kibbutzniks, the news made no impression. "Oh yeah? The dollar fell?"—some people shrugged their shoulders. "Panic in Europe? Really?" These were the only reactions to news that had spread like wildfire to all the world's capitals. The news, announced some time later, that Ordonka was about to start a concert tour of Palestine caused a thousand times bigger sensation. The concerts of great artists are the true sensation around the *kibbutzim* here.

Do I need to say more? At the time when the Wall Street Crash went rolling around the world I did not have a single dollar to my name, nor did any of my family. And yet, even though it didn't affect me personally, it still made a huge impression, the way the news of some great catastrophe does, such as the Japanese navy unexpectedly bombarding Shanghai or the eruption of Krakatoa or the discovery of a sea in Tibet might. On these people here it made no impression whatsoever.

And yet these *kibbutzim* belonged to a people who at that time reacted in the liveliest manner to this same news. Their relations, not just in Warsaw or New York, but also in Oszmiany or Sędziszów, reacted to it as if to epoch-changing news. The words "The dollar has fallen by twenty percent!" tore at the most delicate strings of their souls. But in Emek Israel those same words searched in vain for such strings, perhaps hidden behind others or perhaps by now forgotten. They searched, but found none. As I mentioned before, Jews in Palestine write, speak, and think, not in Yiddish, but in a tongue which had been dead centuries before Latin. The resurrection of Latin today is sheer fancy, but the rebirth of Hebrew is a fact. I ask you, Dear Reader, if you want to use the facts described in this reportage to construct an informed opinion about what is actually happening in the new Palestine, to understand how many sacrifices have had to be made to bring that language back to life.

At this point, I recommend that you give attention to the event described above. It illustrates succinctly, more than a long discussion, how Palestine had changed these people. Well? The different reaction of a Jew from Nalewki, for whom the fall of the dollar must have been a bolt from the blue, and that of a Jew from the Merhavia collective—that's the measure of the change.

17

Only Four Weeks

During my trip to the "orange" colonies, from Tel Aviv and Hadera, I visited fellow travelers whom had I met on the *Dacia*. I found almost all of those I had befriended on the boat. They were separated and split among three different *kibbutzim*, but which lay close to each other. Two of them were still waiting for their land, which in most cases is leased to a group after a few years of working together as hired hands. I was looking forward to the meeting and was received by them like an old friend. But I also made a mistake. Going to the meeting I assumed we would have long discussions about kibbutz life, expected to hear stories of people whose life dreams and philosophies had finally been brought to life. When I arrived in Kfar Saba they had completed their fourth week of work in the fields.

I remembered those hot, lively, complicated discussions conducted in the evenings on the boat. I admired the dialectical skills of those young people. Any discussion with them was ten times the task I would have had back at home. They were almost diabolically skilled at it. Very quick, lofty minds. Pacifism, Marxism, the Trotsky-Stalin conflict, Einstein, Spengler, Coudenhove.[1] An amazing ability to uncouple sympathies and animosities, step back from supposedly universal but in fact only a particular problems, to judge everything from the heights of abstraction. I was hoping for a kind of "earthing," that their abstract loftiness had distilled into a few clear opinions and lessons. However...

I asked Moses Schamroth, my old friend from the *Dacia*, a simple question—did he feel happy now? He smiled in a way that could have served for

---

1   Richard von Coudenhove-Kalergi (1894–1972)—an Austrian Japanese politician, philosopher, great-grandson of the famous Polish socialite and pianist Maria Kalergis; a pioneer of European integration, he served as the founding president of the Paneuropean Union for forty-nine years. (Transl.)

an answer. But then the smile faded. Was he experiencing some ideological disappointment? Well, the disappointment was what they were all experiencing, great disappointment. "Imagine, we came here on the understanding that certain colonist would give us twenty dunams of orange *pardes*, and another—another twenty dunams. The bastards are giving only ten."

This was Moses Schamroth's great worry.

In the course of those few days I spent with them we didn't have a single discussion. It wasn't just that in the evenings they all were very tired: we were all tired, they of course working much harder than I did, of course. It was simply because the old subjects for discussion, which sparked off heated polemics, all receded beyond the horizon of the jobs in hand. Their abstract interests were superseded by the problems of building sheds in place of tents, plans to set up a poultry farm, the surplus of girls, arguments with the colony's employer, or the secret offer of a better deal from someone near Hadera. Their thought horizons were painfully shrunken. Before, Moses Schamroth's mind soared through the universe and measured time in eons. Today, one could say that his perspective had been reduced to six hectares, literarily.

It was an interesting process, which could be called the "peasantrification" of the intelligentsia. These people, irrespective of their formal education and diplomas, were pure intelligentsia: intellectual, brave, and classically impractical in their political thinking and revolutionary theories, and always in search of something to critique. They formed a hotbed in the same way that Russian students' lodgings were hotbeds for the Soviet Revolution, Warsaw's School of Chivalry was for the 1831 November Uprising,[2] and the *Burschenshafts*[3] were for German unification. They frothed with ideas which finally spilled over into Zionism and then, still frothing, flowed all the way to Kfar Saba, where they sank into the sand.

The peasantrification happened overnight. No revolution, no conceptual revision. In principle, Moses Schamroth remained a Marxist and when called upon would confirm his faith in any of his beliefs proclaimed on the *Dacia*. But

---

2   November Uprising (1830–1831)—also known as the Polish-Russian War or the Cadet Revolution, was an armed rebellion in partitioned Poland against the Russian Empire. The uprising began on November 29, 1830 in Warsaw when young Polish officers from the local military academy revolted, with momentous consequences for the British royal house of Mountbatten. (Transl.)

3   *Burschenshafts* (Germ.)—traditional German student fraternities, popular from the nineteenth to twentieth century; they were originally founded in the nineteenth century by university students inspired by liberal and nationalistic ideas, which led to the unification of Germany in 1871. (Transl.)

he just lost interest in them. He does not care so much now. As it turned out, the sheer force of the movement he had chosen to follow sufficed, robbing him of his revolutionary faith in the process. That faith which had bubbled in him since his ghetto days, which had crystalized into a rebellion inside capitalist anti-Soviet society, which would have survived years of prosecution, imprisonment, and police invigilation, now, after four weeks of work in a collective, had fallen flat. Back on the ship, I wondered if Marxism was for the young man a kind of counterweight to a religious belief; I wondered even if some other new idea could outbid his current convictions. It turned out that the strength of the movement he followed himself, unheedful of his revolutionary faith, sufficed. If I bring Moses Schamroth's story up and dwell on it, it's not because this happened only to him. The same process took place in all of them. But Moses Schamroth's path was the longest.

The image of Kfar Saba reminds me of a discussion about revisionism I heard one evening in Emek. There was a time when those people there, too, would have reacted differently to a lecture on fascism and its dangers. Their revolutionary fizz had gone flat too. Totally flat? It seems it certainly had undergone a similar process to the one directed by the laws of physics, the transmutation of energy, or perhaps it simply got "earthed" in the Palestinian soil around orange trees. . . .

It's as if in the course of those four weeks a change of elites had taken place too. Until then, Moses Schamroth had been the specialist and a leader. Now he had taken a step back into the shadow of people who listened to him respectfully as he discussed and lectured them, but who, it turned out, were better with the *turia*,[4] confrontations with the colonist boss, and work management. The finest of the *Dacia's esprits forts* shared his fate. People I didn't notice then—energetic, healthy young men though they were—had stepped forward. Those who'd been everything were not, perhaps, nothing, but those who were nothing had now become truly everything.

Will "those good old days" come back? I don't know. But I suspect they won't. As long as the farming goes on it will produce—albeit different—problems. Ideas do not come back to life. Ideas only change. Once realized, an idea needs superstructure, especially an idea that is nothing more than a certain materialistic, economic doctrine.

---

4   *Turia*—a type of broad-bladed hoe, perhaps used on orange plantations. (Transl.)

18

The Wailing Wall

"Have you been to Jerusalem?" I was asked at one of the *kibbutzim*. "Of course," I said.

"And did you see the Wailing Wall?"

"I did."

"Isn't that funny? You are a Christian and a Pole. I have lived in Palestine eight years, this friend of mine three, these others three and four, and none of us Jews have been to Jerusalem. No time. . . . "

What is the Wailing Wall—the only remaining fragment of the old Temple of Solomon—to the Jews of the Diaspora, if not the greatest, and the only, national and religious holy relic? It's like the crown of Saint Stephen to the Hungarians or the lost royal insignia to the Poles. The old Jew comes to Palestine to stop by the Wailing Wall. That's the first place he goes to. In the *kibbutzim*, there are hundreds of people who have lived in Palestine for years and still have not been to Jerusalem. It takes half a day to get from Emek to Jerusalem.

How should one understand this dragging of Jewish feet, then? How to explain it when one knows what the Wailing Wall means to a Jew? Is it because people nowadays are turning away from religion? No. The Wailing Wall is still the holiest of national holies for Palestinian Jews, perhaps more national than holy. The secularization of the Jews who come to live in the new Palestine does not quite explain it either. The reason lies elsewhere.

I spoke earlier about the amazing phenomenon of revolutionary zeal practically exploding out of the arriving *halutzim* and how it goes all flat after the first few days of working the land. I said it probably transmutes into different kind of energy. In human nature, as in the whole universe, nothing is lost. That energy, that revolutionary zeal, fused with the centuries old longing of Diaspora

Jews, does not, not even at first contact with the Promised Land, change its voltage, direction, or character.

Stanisław Mackiewicz,[1] in his study on the psychology of Soviet society *Myśl w obcęgach: studia nad psychologią społeczeństw sowietów* (Thinking in a Vice: Studies on the Psychology of Soviet societies) writes about the hypnosis, hysteria, and narcotization of society by propaganda during the five-year plan. In a different sense and by different means something similar has taken place here. A *halutz* arriving from the Diaspora follows magnetic attraction to the prospect of rebuilding Eretz Israel. Just like the hoplite of Xenophon's legion longing for Hellas, having roamed the vastness of Asia cried "Thalatta! Thalatta!"—so these people dreamed about *kibbutzim*, building houses, and *moshavim*. These people did not come to Palestine as tourists, they came to work. Feverishly, hurriedly, as soon as possible.

The slogan "Socialism in our lifetime!" which must have been widely heard back home, which for them often had a nice ring to it, changed into the not-quite-fully articulated "We want our Fatherland!" A huge change. For centuries, Jewry waited to return to the land of its forefathers. What's more, Jewry took pride in its waiting, showing that it waited and knew how to wait. For the new generation, though, to wait for Palestine is a disgrace. Yes, nothing less. The apathy of the ghettoes transmuted into the zeal of the *kibbutzim*. One could say that these people sensed the approach of a great, unknown danger, of a coming storm from which they had to run and build a new ark to survive. The love of fatherland, which used to be a form of contemplation, today has no room for contemplation, no time for it.

And there is another thing. The Wailing Wall is reached by descending the narrow, smelly streets of the Arab town. One walks down accompanied by the sneering grins on Arabs' faces. Tens of visitors stand in front of a wall, its old stones scored by centuries. It's a ruin, poor and pitiful, but in its age-old dignity equal to that of the pyramids, maybe even more so. But still—poor and pitiful. A policeman is on duty. Eyes don't wander much higher, for higher there is only an expanse of regular wall, which reminds one that behind it, on the ruins of the greatest glory of Judaism now stands an Arab mosque that Jews are forbidden to enter. On the very spot where Solomon's Temple stood! One should also recall that the regular wall on top of the Wailing Wall was raised by the Jewish

---

1   Stanisław Mackiewicz (b. 1896 in Saint Petersburg, Russia, d. 1966 in Warsaw, Poland—regarded by some as the foremost political journalist in prewar Poland; after World War II, he was the prime minister of the Polish government in exile (1954–1955) before his return to communist Poland in 1956; brother of Józef Mackiewicz, the writer. (Transl.)

philanthropist Montefiore to protect the praying Jews from the stones and rubbish thrown over the wall by Arab urchins.

The Wailing Wall is a symbol of endurance and survival, but as a sacrum it's a typical holy relic of a nation in bondage. Its poverty and pitifulness cause people who have made a pilgrimage to it to cry out their lives of sorrow and contempt. But these are exactly the features that have estranged it from the new generation who are already rebuilding Zion. Those smelly little streets, those Arab sneers, that poverty and ruin, those memories of beatings, and that policeman, whose presence is necessary to secure the peace of the nation standing on its sacred soil—all that stirs up revelation and rebellion in the new people. The sacrum of 2,000 years of bondage remains sacred. But as long as the indignity and contempt of the past is a past and an old nightmare, the Wailing Wall will remain for the young an unwanted sacrum of bondage.

And again—is it strange? For the first fifteen years of Polish independence, our sacred national anthem was a song reminding us of our fate as helots thrown out of our land. It was an anthem of the young, not of the mature, and of the most nationalistic young. It was sung by thousands in the newly independent country, just like the young in rag-and-ruin Russia sing about the revolution which will encompass the Earth or the young in defeated Germany sing about their fatherland's future victories. The conflict about the anthem between the young patriots at our universities was constantly stirred up by the so-called Camp of Great Poland, which insisted on choosing another old song *Rota* for the anthem—*Rota*.[2] The French used to get high on their *La Marseillaise*, we were supposed to delight in the poetry of "No German will spit on our face." . . .

This is of course a digression. I don't want to obfuscate in any way my "study on the psychology of the *kibbutzim*." But it is sometimes useful to compare something foreign with something from one's own backyard, however painful that might be.

---

2   *Rota* (The Oath) is an early twentieth-century Polish poem, as well as a celebratory anthem, once proposed as the Polish national anthem. *Rota*'s lyrics were written in 1908 by Maria Konopnicka as a protest against the German Empire's oppression and suppression of Polish culture in German-occupied western Poland under partitions from 1772–1918. (Transl.)

19

Socialism

Socialism . . .

At the headquarters of the Histadrut Haovdim, I was told: the *kibbutzim* have implemented socialism a hundred percent. There is no private property. Children live, and are brought up, separately, away from their parents.

But in the "rich" kibbutz in Ein Harod, in Yonay's one-room apartment where I was billeted, I saw in the adjoining alcove two sleeping children.

"So your children sleep with parents?"

Yonay was a bit embarrassed.

"You see, we've come to the conclusion that it's better for the older children to sleep with their parents. . . . It's nice somehow. . . . And it leaves more room in the nursery for playtime and the newborn . . . . "

Well, it was not my business to pry. But a few days later, I was visiting another kibbutz, Degania Alef, I think. My guide Hayuta Bussel[1] showed me one of the apartments. In a cramped room, I saw three white-painted children beds. Now I was surprised.

"How is it, comrade? At the Histadrut, I was told clearly that children are separated from their parents from day one and that they sleep separately, collectively, not with family. Yet here . . . "

Hayuta Bussel answered, like an old practitioner who doesn't care much for theories.

"In our kibbutz (and Degania as one of the oldest is a famous one) we came to the conclusion that it is better when small children are brought up and live with their parents."

---

1   Hayuta Bussel (1890–1975)—a historical character, wife of Joseph, the founder of Degania; frequently mentioned in many publications on the role of women in early Zionism. (Transl.)

Kibbutzim are built on, and by, families: "We have a number of families and a number of unmarried singles . . . ," I was informed in every kibbutz I visited. Family here is the basic unit. At a kibbutz which is still in the process of formation there are no families and no children. The older the kibbutz, the more people marry. Everywhere I went, despite the kibbutzniks' young age, this was the case for the overwhelming majority of families.

No one, as yet, has compiled statistics on the ratio of grown-ups to children in the *kibbutzim*. Nevertheless, I could calculate without much difficulty that an average kibbutz couple has three kids. And they are mostly young, have only been married for a few years. Apparently, the British don't like *kibbutzim* because "there, the Jewish population growth is relatively high"—not in accordance with the limits imposed by Great Britain. Large families with many kids are rare, true. But even the Catholic religion states that the main reason for a marriage is procreation. Here, procreation has the added rationale of national interest. Its aim is new fighters and *halutzim* for the new Palestine.

Before these people came here they were often inoculated not just against smallpox, but against a whole school of "eugenics" propaganda. They knew all its arguments and recommendations for birth control. But somehow the "eugenic inoculations" did not catch on, even though living conditions would often make a good argument for them. And many socialist theories made that argument which in Poland is popularly known as "Boy's propaganda."[2] In many *kibbutzim*, people live in real poverty. In all of them there are many children. Married couples (marriage is often, perhaps even as a rule, preceded by a trial period). Childless couples are regarded as "accidents of nature," and they are. Kibbutz couples usually have several children. And this is so despite the fact that many women in the Emek *kibbutzim* have endured and been worn out by years of road building, even though the champions of equal rights preaching that women can do this sort of work just as well as men.

I could not—not then in Degania nor when I saw that all order is based on family, the very same family on which *our* social order is based and which so many collectivities are bent on destroying—I could not shake off the impression that inside Palestinian *kibbutzim* the same process was taking place as in

---

2   Boy—Władysław Boy-Żeleński (1874–1941)—Polish playwright, poet, critic, and translator of over one hundred French literary classics into Polish, including Proust's *À la recherche de temps perdu*. He was a pediatrician and gynecologist by profession, a feminist, and together with Irena Krzywicka one of the first promoters of birth control and women's rights in Poland; he was murdered by the Germans during the so-called "massacre of Lviv professors." (Transl.)

the Histadrut's plans for "proletarian housing": people were simply abandoning Marxist dogmas. Have they gone wrong? They've undermined socialism, perhaps. But they've saved communal life.

***

Another digression, just a thought on the side. The fecundity of kibbutz families is secured and protected by a simple fact: a kibbutz will always provide a new kibbutznik with support; if not this kibbutz, then another, while back in the country. . . . But there is an unmaterialistic reason behind this. It seems to me that these people feel, unconsciously or not, that apart from the sustenance and material support they provide for their children, they will also pass on to them something more, a great idea, certain higher goals to pursue. I doubt if in this respect we have many in our country who have much to pass on. . . .

20

Collective Love

Arriving at a kibbutz late one night, I went straight to bed. I was given a room with four more beds in it. In the morning, I saw that all of them were taken by women. Socialist Palestine was going the way of Soviet Russia . . . ?

I wasn't put in a room with women because of some principle. Nor was it an example of some "Oriental licentiousness." It was simply because there was no other room available. And living a life where the usual means of sexual stimulation, such as books, cinema, illustrations, newspapers, vaudeville, and advertising posters are absent—in such a life the relationship between the sexes is balanced differently.

On my way back to Poland, I travelled with a kibbutznik who told me that in a kibbutz sexual intercourse not based on love is shunned. I knew this and what he told me only confirmed it. Life in a kibbutz is monogamous. It's not rare that perfectly healthy and normal people have to live in total abstinence, as the lack of—let's call it reciprocal partnership—makes sex impossible. The socialist's claim that where there is no money there is no prostitution seems to be confirmed too. Occasional sex of a polyamorous character has given way to monogamy. Which is, however, preceded by a trial period. I can hear someone say it's just sexual friendship, of a kind that is, apparently, quite common in the West, for example among Parisian students where a girlfriend shares her digs with a boyfriend, but such "marriages" are different. If such a "marriage" evolves into a stable relationship it is an exception; in a kibbutz it is a rule. And a solid one.

21

Kibbutz, Kolkhoz, Cloister

While visiting Palestinian collectives one can't help thinking about those other collectives strewn about a much larger area, a thousand-fold larger than that of Emek Israel, Tiberias, and Samaria—the *kolkhoz* of the Union of Soviet Socialist Republics. What are the similarities and differences between the two systems founded at more or less the same time and built on the same Marxist ideas, but established in such unlike circumstances.

The *kolkhozy* were established and function under coercion; the *kibbutzim* by the free will of their members. That's the main difference the Palestinian socialists point out.

It is of course a huge difference, but at the same time a small one. Huge—because a system kept alive by force is only an artificial one and all its official production has to be put down to the strength of the bayonets holding it together. Small—because, ultimately, if we discovered today that the Egyptians built their pyramids out of their own free will and were not forced to by terror, the pyramids would still be the pyramids and the new discovery wouldn't mean a jot to us. But there is *another* difference.

Kibbutz life runs as a socialist scheme, but in that scheme there are parts from which an orthodox Marxist would recoil with horror. In Russia, the *kolkhoz* converted Orthodox churches into village eateries; Ein Harod, the template of a kibbutz, built a synagogue. In Russia, the orthodox communist fights religion, whereas in the kibbutz he is, at worst, an atheist. On many occasions, I heard Yonay's answer repeated by others. When asked about religion, people who do not believe reply that they do not think about it anymore, but that they do not condemn it either—or deny they may return to faith in the future. As for the attitude towards religion, and I looked at it quite closely, I do not think it's any better or worse than elsewhere. Whether

I think that the situation in our Polish Catholic society does not leave much to be desired, that's another question. But if someone asks me about the standard of morality in kibbutz society I will not hesitate to answer that I think it's closer to the ideals we espouse. "What sort of a commune is this," the Bolsheviks will cry out, "which builds a house of prayer and doesn't give a damn, or a 'five-year plan,' for godlessness?!"

But even this, perhaps exaggerated, example does not reveal, just like the point about coercion, the fundamental difference between the communes of Soviet Russia and those of Palestinian Zionism. The difference lies somewhere else: the socialism of the Palestinian kibbutz is just a building block in the economic structure of a new society. This and only this. In Russia, socialism was imposed not only in place of the tsarist system and private ownership, but also in place of all other social ideals, national and religious. Socialist Palestine is simply trying to swap socialism for capitalism. That's all.

One does not have to be all that well read in economic theory to understand the full weight of consequences flowing from that single clear and simple difference. The prescriptions of socialism taken as economic rules only, aimed at improving living conditions, could be changed simply by changing people's expectations. But (Soviet) socialism substituted for other ideas, such as religion. *That* socialism was an entirely different ball game. With every Orthodox or Catholic church converted into a youth club, the tiniest part of Marxist doctrine was laced on the empty pedestal of religious dogma. The questions of children's upbringing in Palestine were answered according to local requirements and the views of the actual decision makers. In Russia, the only point of view on such things was whether a given solution accorded with Marxist theory or not. Those same changes applied here were only variants; the same changes applied there became heresy and called for punishment worthy of treason. A European who does not wash goes dirty; an Arab who does not carry out his ablutions, which are religious commandments, becomes godless.

Which is why in Palestine, when talking about its "socialist part," it is often stressed that in these circumstances, and given the aim of the enterprise, the colonization carried out in the form of *kibbutzim* was probably a more effective tool and more efficient way of achieving them. All agree: capitalism gave us Tel Aviv, socialism gave us Emek. What does this mean? It simply means that socialism has become a tool, one of the tools of the national movement. It has taken place among tractors and incubators. I use these economic comparisons on purpose, for they best highlight the role of socialism in Palestine. And not because I want to belittle its role. What I wrote about Emek or the house-building program of the Histadrut—carried out under the banner "To each worker his own house!"—would quash any criticism levelled at this point. No. All I want to say is that socialism has entered a field where it can achieve more and greater things than anywhere else.

"The Palestinian collective is not based on coercion." In the whole of Palestine, there is not one man who would belong to a collective against his will. People joined out of their own free will. And left in droves too. There is one thing worth pointing out here, a fact that kibbutz people are well aware of. They say: "kibbutz life is hard." What do you need to live this life? Well, strong Zionist and socialist ideals to start with. Others add: a predisposition to communal life. Not all people have them. Each kibbutz has had scores of people who have passed through. Like novices through monasteries.

As a result:

People living in this system today are perfectly aware that, imposed on the masses, it would be close to penal servitude. And they add that humankind simply is not adult enough for these ideals yet. One can also sometimes hear that economic communism is not for everyone: it's a question of individual differences, which have always existed and will never disappear.

At this juncture, we can see that this form of collectivism bears a strong resemblance to a much older one, which has been functioning for centuries and has developed an ability to coexist with its surroundings no less peacefully that Emek with Tel Aviv. And which grew out of prehistoric primal communism into a more elitist form: the monastery. Despite huge differences between a monastery and a kibbutz, the chief one being devotion to God as opposed to a manmade concept, or even celibacy, I would venture the claim that a kibbutz has more in common with a monastery than with a *kolkhoz*.

22

The Jewish Population Catches Up

The rooms in Jerusalem houses are deep, cavernous niches. Their windows are pushed out as far as possible as if trying to protect the interior from the world outside. They are chillingly cold in winter and stifling hot in summer. But deep inside, when neither can be felt, they are peaceful, peaceful with the peace of a museum or a patrician home in an ancient, long-abandoned town. Jerusalem is a town that was compared to a widow's robes long before Christ's death. Her twisting, medieval, narrow streets have often been gutters running with blood that fell like rain. Jerusalem is a town of mourning. The fine dust of mourning, the dead and powdered horror of ages, floats in the air of this quiet room too.

From the oak shelf I pull down at random a gray book. When one is waiting for someone who has just wandered off to other rooms in search of statistics, that's what one does.

> . . . That was the state of the beautiful—in other seasons too—neighborhood of the Staro-Konstantinov[1] district: fertile, undulating, adorned by clumps of trees, which, now devoid of green, gave no sweet shade, but denuded of leaves stood still on the hills like skeletons of groves and flowerbeds. The sky was clear and, as happens in mid-October, the sun shone bright with that melancholy glow of the last

---

1   Staro-Konstantinov—Starokonstantinov, Old Konstantin, a small town in Western Ukraine; from the sixteenth century, it was famous for its fairs and had a continuous Jewish population, largely exterminated during World War II; currently a city in Khmelnytskyi Oblast. (Transl.)

smile one with which one friend parts from another, or a son taking leave of his parents and relatives who are standing on the porch and sending him their last kisses.

Four miles from Staro-Konstantinov, on the left, bogged down on the road. . . .

Something like a soft, moist hand wipes out my images of Palestine, the new and the old, revealing before me my old homeland, now cordoned off. . . . The flaccid pages of the little book speak of the muddy roads of Volhynia, of ladies who have to be carried out of coaches which are bogged down in them, of Szyszkowce and the tenants farms, contracts in Dubno,[2] transports from Odessa . . .

Soundlessly—such deep carpets they have here—my host Yehoshua Farbstein returns. He has the same calm, good-natured smile with which he had welcomed me four weeks previously when I knocked on his door with letters of recommendation; the only Polish Jew sitting on the highest Sanhedrin of the Zionist movement, the Jewish Agency for Palestine (the operative branch of the World Zionist Organization), on which he is the delegate of the religious Zionist party—Mizrahi.

And now he is going to put the flabby flesh of my research on the skeleton of statistics.

"Mr. President," I begin, "one thing that interests my fellow countrymen is the progress of Jewish immigration to Palestine. What are the prospects and possible difficulties? How many Jews can ultimately settle down in the land of their forefathers?"

"Very well, I'm happy to give you all the information. But the answer had better come from the British. . . . "

It doesn't mean he is sending me away to the British high commissioner. Mr. Farbstein hands me two fat volumes—the *Statistical Report for the Mandatory Palestine*, published in Cairo 1933, an official publication compiled by E. Mills, accredited at the British High Commission. And so we begin our perusal:

In the year 1919 (the time of granting the Mandate):

Muslims—457,000

Jews—55,000

Christians—90,000

---

2 Dubno—a historic city in northwestern Ukraine in Rivne Oblast (Pol. Równe) (Volhynian Voyvodship in the Polish-Lithuanian Commonwealth); at the outbreak of World War II over fifty percent of the town's population was Jewish. Most were exterminated in 1942. (Transl.)

In 1931 (the year of the census):

Muslims—750,000

Jews—189,000

Christians—90,000

The figures concerning the other religions remain basically stable with few fluctuations. As for the Jews, I've already heard that in fact the real numbers are much higher. The British themselves told me that in Tel Aviv alone there may be between a few thousand to well over 12,000 "migrants" who have fallen through the census sieve. They are Jews who, because of the restrictive immigration laws, entered Palestine on tourist visas valid for only three months, but who have remained here sometimes for years. Both the British and the Muslims estimate the number of Jews in Palestine at 200,000. Compared with the point at which the British took over the Mandate, that is, in the last fourteen years, the number of Jews here has grown three to four times. But is the figure of 200,000 unchanging? By no means. The spring months of 1933 have been particularly busy, perhaps as never before: the crisis in Europe, Hitlerism in Germany, and the prosperity in Palestine have all contributed. The British statistics, still not finalized, estimate the numbers from between 6,000 and 15,000.

And how many Jews come from Poland?

Here the British statistics are rather imprecise; the old Jewish records, though, speak of forty-five to forty-nine percent. At present, Mr. Farbstein claims, this percentage is significantly higher. (I had this confirmed later at the Polish consulates.)

When I ask this question, Mr. Farbstein turns the pages of the *Statistical Report* and shows me long columns of data: the growth of the Jewish population in relation to the Arab population and, based on that, the predicted growth. Indeed, the *Statistical Report* is worth reading.

Mills states the following:

1) Jewish population doubles every nine years.
2) Arab population doubles every twenty years.

. . . and before these observations sink in with all their consequences, consequences which soon become obvious, he delivers the final conclusion—given the current rates of growth:

3) In twenty years' time, the correlation between the Jewish population and the Arab one will be 1:1.

We put the *Statistical Report* aside. These three calculations blow all the other figures out of the water. Mr. Farbstein unfolds new perspectives for Palestine. The groves (*pardes*), covering 32,000 dunam in 1922 (1 dunam = 1,000 square meters), in eight years grew to 110,000 dunam. And how much more have they grown in the fat years 1930–1933? In 1922, the production of oranges amounted to 1,239,000 crates; in 1932–1933, 500,000. A country the size of the Vilnius region imports yearly £7,000,000 sterling worth of goods. . . .

Above what I am hearing now and what else I have managed to find in those two fat volumes of the *Statistical Report*, above it all floats one thought, namely that from the year 1953 the number of Jews in Palestine will equal that of the Arabs. Perhaps, in that not-so-faraway year nothing of great importance will take place. Yet that meteoric rise, calculated and charted out by the British population specialist, will be passing through each of the 365 days of that year. It will be a historical year: for the first time—not in centuries, but in tens of centuries—there will be a country where Jews will not be in minority. For the first time, in the land of their ancestors they will be able to tell the Arabs—we are on a par. In the year that will come after 1953, for the first time they will constitute the majority.

What is the significance of this fact? I don't know. All statistical calculations are prone to error. All authors writing about Palestine use statistics chosen by a different method. Those I quote are the latest official British statistics. Are they loaded, warped, or falsified? I doubt it, for I don't see any reason why they should be falsified in *this* way. This would be advantageous to the Jews and, as such, would stir Arabs' attention and turn them against the British on whose watch this rise of Israel is happening. No, I don't think so. And whether statistics are farsighted enough to see as far as 1953—that's another thing. But of all the Palestinian statistics, these are the most certain.

One only needs to empathize with the Jews and look through the prism of Zionism to grasp the importance of the calculations in the *Statistical Yearbook*— and they are greater than the Balfour Declaration!

For what was that famous letter of the British minister to the "Dear Lord Rothschild" informing him that "His Majesty's Government views with favor the establishment in Palestine of a national home for the Jewish people"? It was an epoch-making statement for the Jews, yet doesn't it pale into significance when compared to what has been built on it? It is as flimsy as paper compared to the clear, precise, number-based proposition—"The day will come when you will number so-and-so, Arabs so-and-so; it will come in the year 1953"—?

The Balfour Declaration was a historical act. We shall return to it later. It was a ray of hope for political Zionism. It was an unfurling of the great rainbow of hope over all the Diaspora's ghettos. But it was also only one of many promises which between 1914–1918 were handed out left, right, and center by the warring sides. It was an act bearing the stamp of the British Foreign Office, signed by a diplomat, laced with diplomatic provisos, conditions, and understatements. What the *Statistical Yearbook* has calculated today can be checked and revised tomorrow by anyone. What one can see in this blossoming country can be seen by anyone who bothers to come here and see it for himself. These are plain as day, tangible things. The Balfour Declaration needed a Great War and the British victory to become reality. For the predictions of the *Statistical Yearbook* to fail we would need another great war and . . . the defeat of the British.

* * *

How many Jews can still fit into Palestine?

Again, there is no definite answer to this question. Perhaps only as many as can be allowed in. I wasn't given this answer by Yehoshua Farbstein, the Polish member of the Jewish Agency; I arrived at it myself after hearing thousands of other answers to this question. According to neutral assumptions and impartial estimates, Palestine—including Transjordan—can support from three to five million Jews. These are not overly optimistic estimates; they are, if anything, too low.

At present, the population of both Palestine and Transjordan is still relatively sparse. All recent estimates of the land's potential are based on two assumptions: firstly, that Palestine will remain agricultural; and secondly, that there will be no "uneconomic" land improvement. I believe I have already shown what a gross error such assumptions have turned out to be. It's obvious to anyone that Palestine is also developing as an industrial country—just look at Haifa or Tel Aviv or Rutenberg's "great plan," which demolish the seemingly indestructible argument that all industry is founded on coal, which Palestine lacks—! But if the first assumption—that Palestine remains an agricultural economy—is a gross error, the second—that in Palestine no one will be making "uneconomic" investments—is a Big Bertha of miscalculation, it misses the founding principle of Palestinian colonization, which, as we have said before, has never been "economic." The colonization of Palestine cannot be compared to the colonization of America or Australia. Palestine has been colonized "uneconomically" and it is precisely the reason why so many "unprofitable" investments have been made, for they have been made with funds that do not care much for profit. And, incidentally, how many of these "unprofitable" investments have turned out to give a healthy return!

In no other part of this book have I been more anxious not to sound over-optimistic. It is because I am overwhelmed with a feeling I can't properly express—that of a gulf between what I have seen in Palestine and what I thought about it before I arrived here. What I knew and thought then was no different from the thoughts and knowledge of the average Pole. Are things different now? The reader will decide. But if they are different it's because these five weeks of roaming around this country have bent my old line of thinking like steel tongs bend a piece of wire. One has to see Palestine to understand how much truth is in the claim that there is no stretch of land here that can't be converted—sooner or later—into arable land. Today, whole sides of rocky mountains are turned into terraces, filled with soil, and planted with grape vines. On one such mountain the famous Carmel winery is already established. Anyway, if anyone says to me, "Look, Palestine is just sand where even potatoes won't grow," I have the answer ready: "You are right, sir. There is this red sand, which gives a very poor crop of potatoes. But this is also sand that grows oranges and yields profits three times higher per hectare than the best soil of Proszów.[3] And there is a another kind of sand, one on which I've seen a whole new town built."

Well, I won't insist that all this sand will turn into new groves and new Tel Avivs. I only draw a conclusion: namely, that people who have taken whole latifundia of bare land away from the desert—they can take the rest.

* * *

It was after my return to Poland that I read a *Manchester Guardian* report that said ninety percent of the British pharmaceutical industry imports its supplies from the Dead Sea. Palestine Potassium, a big Anglo-Jewish company founded specifically to exploit the mineral riches of that lake, has been working for barely a few years. Apart from Rutenberg's power plant, this is Palestine's biggest industrial enterprise and—just like Rutenberg's plant—it has only just begun production. The riches of the Dead Sea, which have also been undervalued by the English, are inexhaustible. The stagnation in Europe prevents Palestine Potassium developing its natural potential; that's still waiting in the wings.

---

3   Proszów—a thirteenth-century village in the Polish region of Wielkopolska (Greater Poland) on the Silesian border; Proszów is among the most fertile areas in Poland. (Transl.)

These products are still awaiting further development, just like the oranges are not Palestine agriculture's last word. The successful planting of grapefruits, which in the Anglo-Saxon world has become an everyday commodity, has led to the rapid development of grapefruit *pardes*. In comparison with Jaffa oranges, their role is still small, but their future may be huge. While the oranges compete in Europe with the Italian strain (and have won easily) the grapefruit competition will come mostly from California, which, designed primarily for the American market, doesn't pose a great threat. People are talking about grafting the African grapefruit, which apparently is ideal for the soil, with an admixture of salt. Won't plantations around the Dead Sea be the next sure bet? Perhaps. But one thing Palestine can't complain about is shortage of investment initiatives. I don't know if there is a country that has so many. They have concentrated here like the salts, chlorines, magnesium and whatever else might be languishing under the glassy mirror of the Dead Sea. And they push their way towards the date shimmering on the Jewish horizon—the year 1953.

* * *

That evening, I left the apartment of the Mizrachi leader late. I doubt he ever suspected that barely half an hour later I'd find myself in a room where there was not a single copy of the old Korzeniowski novel[4] and where I saw Jewish hopes beginning to dissolve under the weight of the Arab veto.

---

4 Józef Korzeniowski (1797–1863)—born in Brody, today in Ukraine; Polish writer and playwright, bridging late Romanticism and the Balzacian social novel, sometimes employing gothic elements; mostly forgotten by the beginning of the twentieth century. Not to be confused with Józef Teodor Konrad Korzeniowsk, also known as Joseph Conrad. (Transl.)

23

In the Eyes of Young Islam

If Palestine, with all its interest for "the Jewish question," still gets a very superficial treatment in Poland and remains a big unknown, views about the most important aspect of the Jewish settlement in Palestine—that is, "the Arab question"—are even more horrendously ignorant. Our homegrown simpletons see the Arab struggle against Jewish colonization as an extension of their own "war on Jewry." Probably just like at home, they "reason" that the Jews in Palestine bleed money from the people, spoil the race through mixed marriages, take bread away from the workers, dominate trade. They see the Grand Mufti of Jerusalem as nothing less than a leader of the Polish antisemitic organization Obóz Wielkiej Polski (Camp of Great Poland), and it is only the actions of the perfidious Brits that rein in the Arabs who would otherwise show the Jews "their place." This is, of course, a grotesque simplification of their views, but essentially this is the kind of information circulating in Poland. And they are profoundly wrong. A straightforward comparison between Arab antisemitism and Polish, German, or even Russian is a fatal mistake. First of all, Arab antisemitism does not exist of and by itself. What Fr. T. J. Szymański, a historian of ancient Palestine, wrote eleven years ago—that Arabs see Christians as their "brothers" and the Jews as "dogs"—is utter nonsense. The so-called "Arab antisemitism" is nothing else but a part—and not the most important at that—of what Egon Erwin Kisch has described in his fine book *Asien gründlich verändert* (Berlin: Erich Reiss, 1932) as the anti-Europeanism of the peoples of Islam and Asia.[1]

---

1 Egon Erwin Kisch (1885–1948)—Jewish German-speaking Czechoslovak journalist praised for the literary quality of his writing, communist, and anti-Nazi activist, known as the "Raging reporter" after the title of his first bestselling book. (Transl.)

"The Jewish problem, as they describe it in Germany where I studied, does not exist here at all." These were the first words in a short lecture given to me by a young member of the Arab intelligentsia, a graduate of one of the largest European universities, a holder of high office in Palestine. "Just as for us Arabs, there is no such thing as 'the Palestinian problem,' for there is no separate Palestinian nation. Jewish colonization is not our enemy; it is only a tool— one of the tools—in the hands of our enemies."

It is a highly theoretical position, but sounds right, reflecting accurately the general state of affairs. The Arabs say: after our golden era, brought to an end by the Turkish hegemony within Islam, we were a dormant nation, a bit like the Czechs after the Battle of White Mountain.[2] During the Great War, we listened to the English promise of an independent state and revolted against the Turks. We knew the strength of our forces and that of the British, but, alas, we underestimated the extent of their victory, which turned out to be greater and more complete than we expected. We thought the war would end with a compromise that would make space for our own state between the two colonial powers, thanks to which we could sustain our independence, just like Siam or Iran.

As we know, things turned out differently. The undisputed victory of the British (in Europe it was not so complete) allowed them to organize Arabia according to their own plan. The plan was based on the India of the time of the Sepoy Mutiny of 1857,[3] but before it was given the status of a dominion. They created a few states, more or less useful to Britain and more or less dependent on her. Syria was handed over to France. Arabia, united as it was under the Turkish government, was promised independence, but instead was partitioned and offered an "independence" that was a complete fraud. The promises were still too fresh not to cause disappointment. This in turn forced the Anglo-French occupants to look for support among the local population. They started trying to find tribes, religions, races—"minorities"—to whom they could "offer protection" in order to play them against the Arab majority.

It was the first decade of the Arab struggle for independence. The occupants tried all kinds of tricks—in Syria, they found Arabized descendants of

---

2 The Battle of White Mountain was fought on November 8, 1620 at White Mountain near Prague between the protestant Bohemian army and the Catholic Habsburg coalition as part of the Thirty Years' War; decisively lost by the Czechs, it started the centuries-long process of Germanization and erosion of Czech culture which was only contained by the national revival in the nineteenth century. (Transl.)

3 Sepoy Mutiny (1857)—part of an uprising in India against British rule. (Transl.)

Crusaders and tried to make them *les fils dociles de la France,* as the French commissioners called them in their flowery style. The same was done with the Maronites and a few other tribes, and even with purely Arab clans. They found what was left after the Turkish slaughter of the Armenians and turned them into a minority. In Iraq, they "resurrected" Assyrian Christians and played them against Arabs. The same was tried with other small nations. Throughout history, Arabs have not forced Islam on a populace, nor have they forced people to assimilate. Which is why all those small nations and castes have managed to survive here for many centuries. Now the imperialists started to use them as the foundation for breaking up Arabia.

But these plans have failed completely. Failed because the principal part of the population upon which they wanted to build—Arab Christians—has remained faithful to its race. Above all, the Orthodox and Catholic Arabs, less the smaller sects; the other "minorities" are too weak to be politically useful. This maneuver has only consolidated the Arabs.

However, one part of this failed maneuver brought about undeniably significant results—in Palestine.

Support for the Copts and Assyrians, or the creation of an Armenian minority, could never amount to much, like Breton irredentism in France,[4] but opening the gates for Jewish immigration and the proclamation of the Jewish home in Palestine, has achieved the European occupant's goal —it has created a strong and ethnically cohesive population, antagonistic to the native population. The British now have a much easier job governing a country split along national and linguistic lines and they have played Jews against Arabs—and vice versa—as it has suited them and their interests.

Arabia at present—continued my interlocutor—is at a historical point where anti-Arab attacks have been repelled on all fronts. Those who acted as instruments of Britain, now abandoned by her, pay a heavy price [this is an allusion to the Assyrians who were punished with bloody reprisals—Author.]. All our attention and efforts, all the way to Aden and beyond, are now focused on Palestine.

---

4   Brittany, as a historical province on the Armorican Peninsula in northwestern France, has always considered itself a separate, Celtic, nation, and even when it was incorporated into the Kingdom of France it enjoyed relative autonomy; it was only supplanted in the eighteenth century, and was ruthlessly quashed during the French Revolution; Brittany separatism strongly revived at the end of the nineteenth century and peaked in 1920–1940. (Transl.)

Have you seen Akko, Saint Jean D'Acre,[5] opposite Haifa? Perhaps you remember this last fortress, the last piece of land held by the Crusaders, the European occupiers of eight centuries ago? Well, Palestine is now like that old Akko. . . . "

I remember how my interlocutor stopped to think and then said:

"The difference is, those crusades were badly organized, they were limited to taking over the land, not colonizing it. . . . "

Then he continued:

"We have this deep antipathy for Europeans, to your civilization, which we, raised in the West, can see right through. We have a desire to be masters of our own land—we can share it with other nations and religions, but we will not stand for intruders. We will not stand for them most of all because they are instruments of occupiers. . . . "

At this point, I started my interview proper. I asked my Arab friend and his companions, who didn't speak French very well, a few questions and noted their answers practically verbatim.

Question. Hasn't the influx of Jews built up the country economically?

Answer. It has. Undoubtedly it has. Most of all through the import of capital.

Q. Have the Jews had a negative influence in Palestine on Arab spiritual life? I mean, don't the Jews face similar accusations as they do in Hitler's Germany.

A. Here the opinion is somewhat divided. Mostly, one doesn't hear such accusations. Educated people don't make them.

Q. Do the Jews grow fat, as some say in Europe, on Arab injustice? Or, in other words, do Jews exploit Arab workers?

My very correct interlocutors felt rather offended. They considered the question loaded, for it's common knowledge here that the Jewish settlers pay Arab workers better than the Arabs (as is quite often pointed out by the Jews). Eventually, I got a negative answer. There is only one means of exploitation here and that is, if and when more Jews come to settle here and they, as is most likely, hire their own workers.

Q. Is there a threat to Moslem holy places, such as the Mosque of Omar, for instance?[6]

---

5   Akko, also Acre—a city in the coastal plain region of Israel's Northern District at the extremity of Haifa Bay; during the Crusades it was known as St. Jean d'Acre after the Knights Hospitaller of Saint John of Jerusalem, who had their headquarters there. (Transl.)

6   Mosque of Omar—the author may mean either the mosque in the Old City of Bethlehem opposite the Church of the Nativity, or the mosque in Jerusalem, located near the Church of

The answer was again negative, the reason being that the Jews of Palestine are religiously indifferent, or at least focus mostly on cultural or political life rather than religion. On the other hand, the strength of Muslim religious feeling (and Arabia is a typical peasant society irrespective or despite of the effendi and the middle class) is a sufficient deterrent.

Q. Are you afraid that Palestine may become a country where the majority are the Jews?

A. Yes.

That answer surprised me. At the moment, the ratio of Jews to Arabs in Palestine is 1:3.5, if not worse. That means the colonization pressure felt by the local population must be strong.

Q. Do you, gentlemen, see a possibility of reaching some kind of a common position, a Jewish-Arab common cause against the British? The creation of a dual-nationality state, or a canton, a state within a federation?

A. No. Britain's line on Jewish politics, as seen from the Jewish side, is a half measure, but seen from our side it's basically pro-Zionist. A common stance is impossible, Jews themselves don't want it. The Jews are a factor in the Anglo-Arab war, but not one side in a conflict with the Arabs.

Q. If, however, the circumstances developed otherwise, don't you think an Arab-Jewish compromise would be possible? Don't you think that if you cannot overwhelm an enemy, the way you suppressed the Coptic or Assyrian irredentism, then you should learn to live with it?

A. Such a compromise is, of course, theoretically possible, but unrealistic in practice. The only communication coming from the Jewish side is their socialist propaganda among our people. Without passing judgment on its intrinsic merits, that is whether it sincerely aims to improve the position of the working class, the basic fact is that it is aimed mostly at those who politically and financially support Arab self-defense and independence. In other words, it's an activity which effectively undermines the Arab struggle against the enemy. You must admit it's not in fact "an invitation to talk."

Q. To sum up: the Arabs support the fight against the British and exclude the possibility of a compromise with the only force in the country that gives your occupants an excuse for occupation and is capable of the economic liberation of the country. Don't you think that if you follow this path you will have to wait a long time before you reach your goal?

---

the Holy Sepulchre; both mosques are the only Muslim temples.

A. Sure. But just as the Great War got rid of the Turks so another great war may bring about other big changes. . . . "

That was very diplomatically put. . . . I had to adjust accordingly to communicate on the same wavelength. And here the conversation became most interesting.

Q. That's all true. But on the other hand, you also said the Great War swept away the Turks only to sweep in the British. Aren't those who count on another great war worried that it will replace the British with someone else? The Russians, say? . . . Of course, that's just hypothetically speaking. . . . And wouldn't they be even worse than the Turks or the British? Spreading socialism even more effectively than the Jews?"

Now the interview became more a cloak-and-dagger exchange.

A. Those who think like you don't seem to realize that the Great War, the First World War, taught the Arabs a great many lessons, among them this— never allow anyone a total victory or work for anyone's complete defeat."

Our conversation seemed to have arrived at a point where my guests preferred it to remain vague, but its thrust was clear.

Jewish immigration to Palestine before the First World War was met with growing antisemitism. But that was either religious fanaticism or simple envy, which sometimes even ended in robbery. All this changed after the war. Frustrated Arab hopes somehow began to be associated with the massive growth of Jewish settlements, increasing regularly year after year by tens of thousands. The Jew, formerly a religious antagonist, now appeared on the horizon as a national antagonist. If one wanted to lead the Arab masses from religious to national hostility, the Jews provided the perfect footbridge. Especially given that cultural differences in Arab society can be seen as a chasm stretching back centuries.

And yet, how different is the situation here from Poland or Germany?

The Jews in Poland are hated for "obtruding in Polish life"—for "parasitic trade" at the expense of the Poles, for "taking professional space away from their Polish competitors," for their looks even! None of this obtains in Palestine: the Jews do not obtrude in the Arab world in any way. They create their own world. They want to create their own world. There is no point talking about their growing numbers since they are not a burden, neither culturally nor economically. Quite the opposite. Arab antisemitism is an altogether a different animal, different from any other kind of antisemitism, even that of the Germans. Here there is no envy along the lines of "Jews are everywhere; Jews own everything." For what they own wouldn't be here without them. Here we are not talking about antisemitism, but simply about an old tribal hatred, one of those national vendettas like that between the Armenians and the Turks, of the kind whose last remnants in Europe can be observed in Albania or Macedonia. It is a part of the great Arab xenophobia and it is a hatred that is totally blind. If a European travelling through Palestine does not feel he is an object of hate it is only because all of this today is concentrated on the Jews—hardly anything is left for others. The term *giaur* (unbeliever), with all its hateful implications, has been now replaced by the word *Jew*. This deep-seated hatred explodes from within any theories about Palestinian antisemitism, even those held by Arab intelligentsia. "Do you know," they asked me once, "that one airplane could bomb all the Jewish colonies in eight hours flat?"

I asked the Jews if this were the case. They only said: "As far as we know, the Arabs do not have any planes. In Tel Aviv, there is a school for pilots, though, a Jewish one."

This seems to illustrate best the current way these the two nations think of each other.

Arabs in the Eyes of Jews

A French journalist wrote, and our democratic anti-Zionistic press (*Przełom*) happily repeats after him, that Jews prefer not to talk or even think about the Arab question. It's hard to find a more false or ridiculous claim. That the political *nous* of all our big parties could not produce a clear, consistent, and workable approach to the Ukrainian question is one thing, but to say the same about Zionism would be far from the truth. Over the last fourteen "mandatory" years, three distinct conceptions of the Arab question have arisen on the Palestinian horizon. Practically a week doesn't pass without our Jewish press deliberating over this question; the worst antisemite could not level such an accusation against the Jews.

Solution 1—Cantonization:
During the first years of Mandatory Palestine, the first British high commissioner was Herbert Samuel, a Jew, who nevertheless didn't serve Jewish interests all that well. Palestine, which for centuries was a homogeneous country, was divided into two: Palestine proper and the land east of Jordan— Transjordan—where one of the Husseins, Abdullah, was installed as a ruler. The idea was clear, and similar to Hymans's solution[1] to the Polish-Lithuanian conflict in 1921, which was to carve out of the old Grand Duchy of Lithuania an area to be split into two cantons—the Lithuanian with Kaunas and the Polish with Vilnius. Jewish immigration was directed to Palestine proper, banning it under severe penalties from Jordan's left bank, the homogeneous Arab canton ruled by an Arab emir. In this way, it was hoped, the Jewish

---

1   Paul Hymans (1865–1941)--Belgian politician, President of the Leage of Nations, mediated during the Polish-Lithanian conflict of 1920-1922 and proposed a canton-like federation based on ethnic lines. (Transl.)

population would be concentrated in the smaller part of the country—in other words, the contentious problem would be limited territorially.

Solution 2—Socialism:
The Histadrut Haovdim and the Palestinian socialists exercised their forceful influence in this field too. When the creation of Transjordan as a purely Arab country did not end Arab unrest in Palestine and when in Transjordan the Muslim clergy and the Arab nobility took power, the socialists called for the replacement of religious-national conflict with class struggle. The Histadrut began recruiting Arab workers. They began to organize them and collaborate with them in strikes against Arab employers.

Yet, despite huge efforts, the results have not been impressive. Collaboration between the two national proletariats against the propertied classes does not exist and, if compared to the Arab-Jewish antagonism, it is practically nonexistent. And lastly, giving Marx to the Arab masses in place of Mohammed is no guarantee that Arab socialism, instead of joining forces with the Jewish proletariat, will not at some point develop into an Arab Hitlerism, which combines socialism and nationalism. This would be a very dangerous turn for the Jews.

Solution 3—Collaboration:
While Palestine was torn by national conflict and at the same time growing rich, Transjordan remained the sandy stretch it had been from time imme-morial. However, Transjordan also had at its helm one of Hussein's sons and, of all those sitting on Arab thrones, he is undoubtedly an exceptional individual, the ablest of them. Abdullah understood perfectly that the fur-ther development of his country is impossible without Jewish collaboration, which could provide Transjordan with the capital to change its swathes of sand into *pardes*. During the spring session of the Royal Council earlier this year a motion was tabled—to allow Jews to purchase of land in Transjordan.

Yet today this option is, in effect, history. In the face of the huge outcry of the Palestinian Arabs and the weaker resistance of some in Transjordan, which was not without the very active support from the British, the negotia-tions between Abdullah and the two Jewish leaders Farbstein and Newman, the advocates of this solution, did not yield fruit and the motion at the Royal Council was rejected. The gate to Transjordan, where there are still old Zionist colonies going back to Turkish times, has been shut. It is a detail, a moment in the life of a political cycle. No one doubts that sooner or later the gate will open again. In the face of the grinding poverty there, and the fact that the price of land will rise to Palestinian levels when Transjordan opens up to Jews—which means that the value of a landowner's estate will rise seven- to tenfold—the anger of Palestinian Arabs will in the end prove insufficient. Anyway, that anger is unlikely to prove a viable force. In addition, there is a now an active and influential faction which at every opportunity manifests its sympathy for the Jews, and Abdullah has broad-based national support.

While considering this purely practical solution, another suggests itself: after fourteen years, one thing in Palestine is certain—all the Arabs' attacks on Jews have failed and so have all the Jews' attacks on Arabs. The only beneficiary in this fight has been Britain. Fourteen years have shown that neither forcing the Arabs out of Palestine nor expelling the Jews is possible. Furthermore, the only capital that can be invested in the country (apart from exploitative British capital) is Jewish capital. And, finally, claims of a "Jewish threat" to Muslim's holiest of holies is just as lacking in substance as is such a threat to Christian holy places. The Jews who emigrate to Palestine are simply doing so for different reasons.

Solution 4: Arab Catholicism:
I still remember how moved I was when in the Nazareth basilica I could not find on confessionals any labels other than in Arabic.[2] That odd feeling of the church's vitality, her inexorable progress. . . . When the first of the Great Thursday sermons on Gethsemane was given in Arabic by an Arab Franciscan;[3] when on a morning in Haifa I saw a little church filled with a swarm of white Bedouin kaffiyehs and red fezzes. I remember the odd feeling when in the house of some Arab Catholics I had to listen for an hour about how they, having converted to Catholicism, had ceased to be Arab and become "cultured Europeans" and how they had "nothing to do" with "all those out there." I thought then, not without certain chagrin, that back home, not in the faraway eastern lands, but in Słonim,[4] other religious missions

---

2   Nazareth basilica—the author probably means the Church of the Annunciation, also known as the Basilica of the Annunciation, a Roman Catholic temple which, according to legend, is built on the actual spot where the archangel Gabriel appeared to the Virgin Mary and told her that she would bear the Son of God, Jesus—the event known as the Annunciation. The old church the author is referring to was demolished in 1954 and replaced with a modern building. (Transl.)

3   Great Thursday—Christian holy day falling on the Thursday before Easter; it commemorates the Washing of the Feet and the Last Supper of Jesus Christ with the Apostles. (Transl.)

4   Słonim—a historic town in the Grodno District in prewar eastern Poland; home to a significant Jewish population, but also other ethnic minorities including Muslim Tartars; now in Belarus. (Transl.)

don't just awaken but create new nationalities, while in the vast space of the Middle East. . . . But this fact, though frequently observed, is an exception here. For Catholic Arabs did join the Pan-Arab movement. Having rejected Mohammed as the messiah, they nevertheless revere him as a national genius. This has happened perhaps against or behind the backs of Catholic leaders, but it has occurred. I have a feeling that Arab Catholicism has greater things to accomplish now than ever before in this land which has traditionally been hostile to it and this will occur through its full incorporation into the movement of national revival.

A similar case applies to the Jews. There exist great if only imagined plans for merging Zionism with the Pan-Arab movement, of intensifying Jewish immigration not just to Palestine but to Egypt, Syria, and other parts of Arabia. Independence cannot be achieved without capital or an educated civil service. Arabia does not have the former and very little of the latter; Jews can supply both. Today the only active Jewish prejudice is against the Arabs; tomorrow it can be replaced by an equally active and unrestrained hostility towards the British.

These are difficult issues. To overcome them, the Arabs have to understand the benefits union with Jews can bring them, and the Jews have to understand that Arab socialists are not the only ambassadors of the Arab cause and are devoid of power and influence anyway. The decisive voice belongs to the Great Mufti and the people close to him. This not an optimistic conclusion to be sure, but it's based on reality. An enemy with whom one shares common interests, is an enemy one can make a deal with. Talking to anyone else is just a silly delusion: it is as if when negotiating with Russia today one would talk to Kerensky or the monarchists. Still, I have a feeling that the possibility of such talks in Palestine is ripening on both sides. There is a view that neither Jews nor Arabs possess a sense of statehood. Farbstein and Newman's negotiations with Emir Abdullah seem to contradict this.

25

Christian Jerusalem

The cellars of every old house in this town sitting on arid mountains are dug deep into the rock to provide water cisterns; for months on end, the lower rooms are filled with unwholesome, dank cold. But that's how it must be. When, unexpectedly, to the joy of the whole street, a swift rain passes by, the stone gutters on the flat roofs will carry it down along the walls straight into those cisterns. Their deep, empty caverns will start filling up. They can hold cloud-bursting storms. This town where water is rare and precious has created in its bowels a water-retaining system capable of taking in whole rivers.

Something similar happens to the pilgrims. Jerusalem is small, short not only of water but also of houses and people. But at least it rests assured in the knowledge that a huge stream of people—tens and tens of thousands of them—will wash up at its doors, and every year they are ready to receive this stream. Just like the cisterns hewn out of the rocks, big hospices and hotels have risen above the rocks, flophouses and palaces and hovels. They were built by God-fearing people and speculators, Catholics and Protestants, countries, monastic orders, Muslims, and Jews. Since yesterday, parked outside the grand King David Hotel, a silvery-blue Hispano-Suiza has been parked, with a registration plate bearing the coat of arms of the House of Capet and Stewarts and Bourbons, and of Castile and Aragon, the emblems one remembers from museums and keystones that lock the ribbed vaults of medieval chambers. The weary traveler who arrived in the car is heir to no longer existing kingdom, long superseded in unified Italy. But at the foot of the Mount of Olives there is not even one Ford. There, by the high white wall of the Orthodox monastery, people for whom not only is the King David Hotel too expensive, but even the cheapest hospices, camp. Or for whom there is no room in the Holy City. They came here thinking it would be alright, somehow.

Or rather, came without thinking whether or how they would find any lodging. The trouble is, Jerusalem is now in the grip of a "cold snap," which not only fills the old cisterns with rainwater but torments the people sleeping rough on the slopes with cold and rain. There is nothing more piercingly cold than the coldness of night on this barren slab of the Mount. Men lie next to each other in rows tighter than the white tombstones in the cemetery descending in terraces down the slope into the Valley of Josephat. When the cold dew of the night keeps them awake, perhaps they think about that other night, about cold sweat and blood like dew on that other brow, in the grove on the Mount of Olives, that night. . . .

They show us a narrow, arduously climbing little street in the Old City. The street is almost completely made of steps flanked by windowless walls on both sides, as if it were about to be squeezed and smothered by the old Arab hovels. They show us this street and say—"Via Dolorosa." And, instantly, it stops being one of thousands of streets in this unique labyrinth of a town. And then we find everything: bordering on the noisy Arab bazaar is the Franciscan chapel where the Cyrenean was told to pick up the cross. . . . White courtyards, white and myrtle green, a house church put on the spot where Pilate passed his judgement. Following in the holy footsteps, each station is marked with a church or an altar. Like strong muscular branches they push through the thicket of Arab houses of Jerusalem, which by now have covered every square inch of the bald rock of Golgotha. One wanders around here, stumbling anew on the old familiar, recognizing afresh the well known. Until one gets to that square, a small square, not bigger than the one in front of our Saint Anne Church in Vilnius, which separates it from the street. But in this compact, tightly built city it creates the impression of a recklessly opened space. The square falls in two wide steps towards a heavy building with a Romanesque arch for entrance. And then they say: it is here. But one already knows. And then they repeat: this church contains the place of execution and also the tomb. They repeat. It's one's first time here and yet one bridles inside—I know! I don't have to be told, that this—is here.

All those Stations of the Passion, which the Arab ghetto has not been allowed to overgrow, now, even before the crowds get even bigger, are visited by procession after procession, one group of people after another. All kinds of people: all nations, all ages, all social classes. And all faiths and denominations: I met Germans, Lutherans who were looking for their fellow pilgrims lost somewhere on the way (found again of course, back in their hospice). Next was a French or Belgian group, led by a French Catholic priest. The Germans followed them, listening even more avidly than the others to the words spoken in a foreign tongue. At each holy place, they repeated the words of a foreign prayer. Doing this, they probably thought they were the only ones and the first, but this sort of thing happens here all the time, and has done since the beginning.

A journey to Jerusalem is expensive, very expensive. The poor who are here have not come from afar. These who have, and those who are still expected, are people of means at least, or rich. It is striking to see so many thinking faces, striking that particular expression on their faces. All the social elites gather here.

It made me recall that old expression: "The ardent faith of simple folk"—a saying coined at a time when the weakening faith of the upper classes was contrasted with the strong faith of the peasants. It was coined and entered the mainstream, but it seems to be less relevant now. At least in the countries whence the pilgrims come today. For they are all growing stronger again, all and each of them a stark denial of that old, outdated saying, which took hold in the lifetime of one generation. These people now are the avant-garde of a new generation, which will fish that saying out of the mainstream and throw it into the shallows, which have been so successfully navigated in the past by the church of Saint Peter.

* * *

When thinking about the great, famous churches of Europe, an image of crowds comes to mind, of gaping tourists wandering aimlessly with their binoculars and Kodaks and "preserving" their "impressions." In Jerusalem, there are also crowds. In every church, at every holy place there are lines just like Soviet Russia's breadlines. But here there are no "tourists." Which is odd, for everything here deserves such a collector of impressions. It's as if, due to the saintly mood prevailing here, the high commissioner has banned tourism. And it would be perfectly understandable. People undergo a spiritual experience here. Everything feels different here. One would probably have to dig up a few meters of the pavement that has grown like a carapace, like rust, like a patina over the rock, to touch the actual rock and feel it as it was 1,900 years ago. It would take days of shelling to blow away what has been built over those nineteen centuries on Mount Precipice. But here we are, thousands of people have come and, without pickaxes or cannons, revealed Golgotha anew. For them, it is as of all those buildings aren't here. There is only the history of His death.

* * *

In the evenings, cold Jerusalem evenings now, in the great halls of the hospices and the high naves of the churches, the gathered crowds receive their retreat teachings. Their daylight pilgrimage to holy places, heated into a liquid alloy of emotions, is now cooling and hardening into new molds. I think that's the nearest I can get to describing what I see happening to these people. It may be a bit literary, even banal, but with all that it is true. And that's what I want to convey. It's like melting broken-up, rusty scrap and changing it into the glowing sheen of new metal. The pilgrims to this holy city are just such a new alloy. Here one finally understands how the two words—"fire" and "faith"—blend together. Yes, here faith is fire.

Nineteen Centuries after Pilate: A Night in Gethsemane

It was already dark, even on Jerusalem's flat roofs, when we began our descent into a curved, slanting alley. We came around a corner into Solomon Street, a narrow, zigzagging lane which, when seen from the towers, looks like a loose, knotted rope laid between two old gates knocked through the walls, the walls which Solomon fastened around the old town. There was still traffic, but the dark shops of the bazaar were already bolted shut. There was traffic and the light of street lamps and shop lanterns, hung under the arches, which completely veiled the sky above. The Via Dolorosa was dark and packed with crowds.

It cuts right through the old Jerusalem from east to west. Cuts and falls away down in a cascade of worn-out steps, lower and lower. We follow in Christ's footsteps. And so we pass the chapel standing on the spot where Simon the Cyrenean carried Jesus's cross; we pass the Praetorium and the place of the flagellation. It is totally dark. All the little streets to the left and to the right are empty. Down our street a mass of people marches on. Single, in groups, and in pairs. At the bottom of the street, at the feet of the tall, tightly packed rows of houses, it is all black. One can barely distinguish the contours of human figures, the countless figures amidst the flow of marching feet. I lost sight of people who walked in front of me. Everyone seems to be lost in this darkness, but no one is even trying to find a way out. The crowd flows down into the darkness, all the way down. As if on this young Thursday night we were all descending into some old catacomb. The crowd is thickening. I can tell by the growing murmur of feet, the frequent bumping into fellow marchers and the slowing of the march itself. Something in this scenery, the darkness, and the descent, vaguely brings back a memory from afar. Once, along similar back alleys, the people of Trastevere and Suburra[1] flowed to the catacombs for nightly lessons and feasts of brotherly love. Yes, there is a similar scene with Marcus Vinicius, Croton, and Chilon, and with Peter and Paul in Tarsus in Sienkiewicz's *Quo Vadis*.[2] "Quo vadis? Quo vadimus? Getsemani, vadimus hodie. . . ."[3] We are going to Gethsemane.

We are now outside the city walls, the crowd spills out, wider and noisier. The row of lights in the distance marks the line of the tarmac road. The drone of passing cars hangs in the air as they drive past one after another, one after another. Their lights sweep over us as they coast down the slope of the Mount of Olives: here, following the modern, comfortable British road, those in Buicks and Chryslers and taxis make their pilgrimage. Before us, bathed in lights, rises the white-golden facade of the basilica where once Gethsemane stood. It is a brightness framed in the blackness of the mountain behind it; this is our goal. Flowing from Jerusalem are two streams of people—one coming down Via Dolorosa, the other down the rumbling road. Here they meet.

A new, clean, brightly lit church. Lit and full. Faces—Anglo-Saxon, Italian, Bavarian (or Prussian?), Slav, but that's only a half of them. They are thickly interspersed by white Bedouin kaffiyehs with their black agals, the ropes holding them in place, with a good sprinkling of Arab red fezzes and the black faces of Ethiopians. Some Chaldeans, Copts, Armenians, and others, and many different others. One feels lost. . . .

At the altar, aglow with the light of yellow candles, the priest reads aloud the Gospel, verses from Luke, Mark, Mathew, and John. He reads very slowly, pausing after each word, to make the Latin more accessible to those who only know enough of it to follow the verse in their own little books. When he comes to the third, one realizes it is not just a reading of the Gospel, that it is all like a huge tribunal, gathered centuries later, revisiting the scene of the cataclysmic crime. We are in situ of where the olive garden of a suburban farm once stood, where one late spring night Roman soldiers and Temple guards entered. And so now, one after the other, the four who were at the scene, nineteen centuries later, pass on to us their witness.

"Ave Maria, gratia plena, Dominus tecum,"[4] repeats the chorus of people, fingering the beads of their rosaries. Everyone is praying. It is as if they are

---

1   Trastevere and Suburra—populous districts in the ancient city of Rome. (Transl.)
2   Sienkiewicz's Quo Vadis – a popular novel about early years of Christianity in ancient Rome; it won its author, Henryk Sienkiewicz, Nobel Prize for Literature in 1905. (Transl.)
3   Latin: "Where are we going? We are going to Gethsemane today." (Transl.)
4   Latin: "Hail Mary, full of grace, the Lord is with thee. . . ." The first lines of a traditional Christian prayer to Mary, mother of Jesus. (Transl.)

trying to fasten onto these words, the smallest of them, words of prayer worn out by everyday use. It all follows a rhythm, like working together. Together and focused, not one word can be dropped, no hand can grow weak and fall away. It is like carrying a heavy beam on a building site, too heavy for a single individual. This nightly prayer feels like a group working together on a common task, like a work gang. It is as if they are slowly lifting, higher and higher, a massive weight bearing down on them—a weight to which they are shackled and bound.

We are listening to the first lesson. No one who has just arrived understands it. Before the altar stands a crowd of Bedouin keffiyehs and the red fezzes of Arab Catholics, listening to a Franciscan priest speaking in Arabic. One has to find a way through the rustle and rumble of words to keep up with the preacher. We know what he is preaching, we are listening. After him, comes a Spaniard, and after the Spaniard a Frenchman. The lessons will continue all through the night. But I am leaving, and a short while later I am at a small, dark garden. Muslims, for whom life on this earth had a transient value, protected trees. The lamps reveal eight olive trees in the dark—old, more than old, wild like a lone pear tree in a field. Tradition has it that it was here that He prayed. Whence He was led by those who came from the city to bring him before the Sanhedrin.

✳ ✳ ✳

On my way back from Gethsemane, over Kidron, which separates the city from the Mount just as it did then, over Kidron and the Valley of Josaphat, white with tombstones during the day, a terrifying starless dark night now hangs. People return in small groups, no crowds, the road feels empty. The city is dead quiet; night in Jerusalem has the true silence of mourning. A small group passed me by, talking in a language that was probably not even Arabic. Seen from the foot of the city wall, Gethsemane is only a tiny white spot. Slowly, to the right of the bulk of the Mount of Olives, a ridge of mountains in the far distance begins—just—to separate itself from the paling sky. At their feet billow clouds of heavy white mist. They rise from the Dead Sea, beyond which, over the mountains of Transjordan, climbs the sun.

Sleep comes fast and hard, but uneasy, in fits and starts, like a bad dream. Something weighs me down that's heavier than tiredness; I feel as if have been hypnotized. I want to close my eyes, turn them away from the big window of the monastery, away from the pale sad morning of Good Friday.

27

The Way of the Cross

Since the morning, nothing but rain and that awful wet cold, which comes over Jerusalem the moment the sun disappears. And from early morning processions on the Via Dolorosa heading for Golgotha. I get to the first Station of the Cross. It's a street, only a street, at which the building of the old Praetorium stands, whiter than the others. But today I'm only passing through here: by the Chapel of the Crown of Thorns, then that of the Dungeon, and the one just before that, where the flagellation took place. All the little chapels, flooded with people since the morning. One can hardly comprehend the power it has over people, the strange drive which takes hold of one at dawn when getting up and ready to be "on time."

I joined a group of Spaniards. I understand very little of the evocative words with which the *conducilore*, a Franciscan, reminds us at each station what took place here nineteen centuries ago. But of course I understand enough. Of those matters, too heavy, too grand, for which even Latin, so beautiful and powerful in its simplicity, is too pale and too weak—the nearest to capturing them is the sound of Iberian words, Romance and yet non-Roman. They have something in them which no other languages seem to possess and which seems to be most needed here, on this true Way of the Cross, and which is otherwise lacking—the horror, the stifling of the voice, and throat-gagging pain when talking about what happened here. It's not sorrow; there is no pious, good-natured, and resigned sighing, such as normally accompanies processions around the fourteen stations in a little parochial church, as if telling the beads of rosary. All that is missing here—what is here and seems wholly natural—is a sense of great distance, of two great distances, of Time and of Space.

The crowds are growing thicker, the rain is falling more heavily, we are slowing down. We have just passed the place of the first fall under the weight of His wooden cross, and then where He fell again, and where the guards pushed the Cyrenean back into the crowd. In this street, climbing up all the way to the summit of Golgotha, crowned by the Crusaders with a church, there are now five maybe seven persons, marching side by side. Station after station. Every step gets us closer to the tomb. It is so strange, that as we move from one station to the next, from one holy marker to the next, bit by bit we are leaving ourselves, the selves of our time and age, and becoming more part of that time and place. Every year in Naples, during mass, the dry blood of a sixth-century martyred bishop kept in an ampoule becomes liquid. But here, and now, something greater is happening. Apparently a simple thing, the kind which we hear from the pulpit of the smallest, remotest parish, or read in the most naive of prayer books—nothing separates us from the Lord's Passion now. An awful tiredness is seeping into our thoughts and prayers, the deathly exhaustion of the condemned man led to the place of execution, the hostile curiosity of the clamoring mob, and the powerlessness of the few, the all-pervasive blessed horror of the moment. It seeps into us and fills us. It seeps in with old memories and images from the Gospels faded over the centuries. It is so gray and brittle and washed out, like that scrap of rust at the bottom of the crystal ampoule in Naples. And at the same time—No! It stirs and swells in us, rises ever more powerful, and bursts forth with the fresh red of the still living, newly spilled Blood.

* * *

All the pilgrims have now passed through a narrow passage under the arches into the small courtyard before the Church of the Holy Sepulchre, built by Godfrey of Bouillon. I do not know why I was left behind, alone in the street. Somehow I lost my Spanish group, then a German, and then another, followed by a black group—who knows, anyway, how many different peoples have passed here? At the end of the Via Dolorosa, there is more room now and it looks just like another narrow, dirty street. Veiled women, like everywhere here, carry precious water in black skins and old petrol cans, slipping on the wet, muddy stones. Everything is gray and dirty. And yet one is stuck to the spot, looking at these thin stones of the Arab street, trodden out of shape, slippery with dirt, almost black. My eyes are searching for the marks and signs which are no longer here, which disappeared a long, long time ago and which one not only knows but feels still mark the road to Calvary with irremovable seals of martyrdom.

The Way of the Cross in Jerusalem on a Good Friday is a tragic reliving of a different way, tragic but uplifting. The Church of the Holy Sepulchre, which covers both the tomb and the place where He was hung on the Cross, is in itself an image of horror. Terrible beyond words, unbearably sad. What is happening today can easily be a part of some Soviet propaganda film about religion.

The church was built by Godfrey de Bouillon on the site of the former Byzantine basilica. All that is standing here was built by the Crusaders, at a time when the knights of the West came to protect the holy places. They left behind, standing to this day, the wonderful Romanesque arches of the facade, truly beautiful in their simplicity. Someone proudly told the Turks that the Church stands not only on the rock but also on the steel of the knights' swords. Sultan Omar took the hint and his new, also beautiful, mosque was raised on the rubble of another temple, one no swords would come to claim—the Temple of Solomon. But in the nineteenth century, the pillars of soldiers' steel were covered with Greek gold, which by now has filled to the brim the whole church.

Through one deal after another, one treaty after another—and at the time when St. Petersburg could put pressure on Istanbul—Calvary, the tomb, and all the other treasures of the Crusaders passed into the hands of Orthodoxy. But let us draw a discrete veil of silence over this new Reconquista in the interest of Christianity. And let us do it mercifully, for that same opulent, gold-filled Church is now scourged not only by what is being done to it by the Bolsheviks, but also by what is happening to all the holy treasures it took into possession.

In the great rotunda, under the dome, in the center of the church, stands a four-meter-high construction of pink-and-brown marble slabs; they stand above the cave hewn from rock which Joseph of Arimathea had prepared for his tomb.[1] The chapel is Roman Catholic and baroque in style, but the entire upper part is covered by many, artistically poor but very tightly packed holy pictures, all Orthodox. The pictures are lit by scores of lamps and candles, making the walls black with soot. To me, it looked, I don't know exactly why, more like

---

1   Joseph of Arimathea—according to all four canonical Gospels, Joseph of Arimathea was the man who assumed responsibility for the burial of Jesus after His crucifixion. The Gospel of Matthew suggests that the burial was undertaken speedily, "for the Sabbath was drawing on" and that Jesus's body was laid in Joseph's own tomb, prepared earlier for himself (Matthew 27:60). (Transl.)

a Buddhist temple than the wondrous Lavra of Pechersk.[2] I could not recognize the Orthodox style I thought I knew. Nor could I recognize the Orthodox faithful. It was just before one of their services and the church was full, frothing with loud talk and laughter. Everyone laughed—the blacks, the women, the Arabs swathed in their *thawbs*. On the floor lay mats on which they were happily picnicking, their backs resting on the tomb. In some places, food was being warmed up on small burners. At the Coptic chapel, nestled in the tomb's wall, children were running up and down from post to post, admired by their proud mothers. The air stank of broad beans, fat, fish, and olives, like Arab stalls in a souk. I was looking for praying faces. I found none.

I remembered the true Orthodox beauty in the Troitskii Sobor,[3] the simultaneously proud and humble beauty of the Byzantine style and liturgy. I saw pictures there which were not tawdry and people who did not go there to see a free show. At the tomb here one would think they were different people. But they are not.

"Greeks," one Russian *batiushka* said scornfully. Yes, they were mostly Greek and Syriac Orthodox. They spend the whole night here, in the church, till dawn. I was there at night when the crowd was awaiting their service, the ceremony of the Holy Fire. They say it's an old pagan custom. And it seems that for these people it is the culmination of Holy Week. It was clear to me these people were pagan. It is not a cultural difference, not just a liturgical difference, or a difference in dogmas. It is simply an expression of a different faith. They are pagan, following Christian rituals. It may be my personal Catholic antipathy for Orthodoxy, a liturgical envy. Perhaps. One could say I am showing here a journalistic proclivity for a paradox. But if you could only see what was going on in that church, on those holy days. . . .

$$* * *$$

Over this most pitiful, most abused of all churches hangs yet another curse. It's not an accident that under its roof meet all of the main faiths. Its every corner gapes with a kind of homeless orphanhood. Its naves are divided and carved up by boundaries, time is broken up into hours, some for these, some for others.

---

2   Pechersk Lavra—also known as the Kiev Monastery of the Caves, a historic Orthodox Christian monastery; since its foundation as the cave monastery in 1051 the Lavra has been a preeminent center of Eastern Orthodox Christianity in Eastern Europe. (Transl.)

3   Troitskii Sobor—Trinity Cathedral in Saint Petersburg, Russia; a late example of the Empire style, built 1828–1835. (Transl.)

In this sharing out of the Christian inheritance, one is painfully reminded of the Roman soldiers quarrelling over the Robes of the Condemned.

* * *

The English policemen keep order over the crowd pushing into the *aedicula*[4] and the small chamber of the tomb. One enters it and stops before a white, marble slab, kissed smooth by visitors, the people camping in the church. It covers the rock-carved hollow of the tomb. And then something happens, as if beyond the wall of the *aedicula* there is no church filled with the clamor and racket of people arguing about places, the quarrelling, the joking, the eating, and the sleeping. As if there were none of those divisions, those schisms, and arguments now arbitrated by the bored British who have replaced the Turks— all that ceased to be!

* * *

After a while, an Orthodox warden of the tomb gives a sign: time to leave. Back on the church's floor everything is as it was. Milling crowds, one has to push hard to get through, an Arab offering a mat in a "loggia" arranged in the arcades around the rotunda. There are thirty-two of those loggias, each a narrow hutch already packed with people. The asking price is half a pound for the night per person; the Arab drops it to twenty piastras. That means going down from fifteen to six zlotys. "Très curieux, très curieux," he assures me. Some tourists are taking photos with a magnesium flashlamp. At the exit, Arab wardens keep warm by a coal grate while playing a quiet game. From the chapels on the upper floor comes out a throaty yodeling, to my ear half wild. But now it is as if I am separated by a wall. That wall.

---

4   *Aedicula*—a small shrine in ancient Roman religion; here one built over Christ's tomb inside the Church of the Holy Sepulchre. (Transl.)

28

Resurrexit

The great holy Eucharist, celebrated outside the tomb's entrance at a portable silver altar, is coming to an end. It's a light, sunny day, the people are different. The ceremony is quiet, more dignified, contemplative; a pious silence hangs over it.

The church is overflowing. German pilgrims stand next to the Polish, the Italian next to the French, Spanish, English. When the organ music stops the silence is total. The mass continues, then the Resurrection and the procession. Led by the *Kawas* guards dressed in Oriental fashion, whose iron-shod staffs resound heavily on the flagstone floor, it flows through the crowd and around the tomb three times, dazzling with the white of surplices and the gold of chasubles.

Te Deum. The air, gray with frankincense, quivers with the triumphant song of victory, the certainty of victory, the sweet joy of victory. *Resurrexit sicut dixit.* Alleluia, alleluia. The Via Dolorosa, Good Friday, and those three days of the Holy Week all burn together with the incense and scatter around the world on the strains of victorious hymn. The bells of the churches toll, Saint Francis', Saint Bernard's, on Mount Zion and on the Mount of Olives. They ring louder and stronger, *urbi et orbi.* On this bright Sunday morning, the peal carries over the white rocks and green hills and the farthest stony field roads of Jerusalem. *Resurrexit, resurrexit, resurerxit.* The old olive trees on Gethsemane listen to the old news.

So Many Different Roads: "Das Wirkliche Deutschland"[1]

On the fifth day of our trek across northern Palestine and its colonies, on which I set off with my companion, a young Jew from Poland, Arie Buchner, we were joined by a third fellow hiker. We met him early morning on our way out of Tel Or; our greetings were drowned in the roar of the Jordan crashing into the open chasm of turbines that churn power for Rutenberg Station. He was young, at most twenty-three years old, on his way to rejoin his comrades at a Zionist kibbutz near Tiberias. He had nothing of the typical heavyset Palestinian *halutz* about him. He had been in the country barely a year and hailed from Berlin. Meeting him was a surprise, at least for me, not only because of what was going on at that time in Germany (April 1933) but also because until then I had met very few German Jews here. We spent half a day together, marching side by side right through the middle of the Jordan Valley.

It turned out that our new comrade knew Poland. He had been there on an excursion, which took three weeks and covered Warsaw, Vilnius, and Białystok. What was even more interesting was that he also stopped by at small, as he put it, settlements, of which he mentioned Kutno, Sochaczew, Nowe Miasto, and Mława.[2] That really surprised me—what on earth brought him to Mława, probably the first ever foreign tourist there?

---

1 Germ.: "The Real Germany" (Transl.)
2 Kutno, Sochaczew, Nowe Miasto, and Mława—small towns in central Poland, well known before World War II for their large Jewish populations. (Transl.)

"Wir suchten das religiöse Judentum."[3]

Thus began the story of the young Jew. It wasn't a broad, soul-searching flow like the Russian confessions I've heard so often before; the narrative was driven by one thought only, namely to make this stranger, who had come to Jordan to learn about what was being undertaken in Palestine, understand why a Palestinian kibbutznik, socialist, and Zionist had to walk so many different roads before finding this last one.

The story revealed many things I had already anticipated. The young man bore an air of affluence and good education, and the look of what they call in Germany "von der guten Kinderstube."[4] The story confirmed that his *Kinderstube* was in Berlin, in the family home of a rich bourgeois industrialist for generations rooted in Brandenburg. The father died during the war on the Western Front, as a result of a poison attack. The widowed mother inherited a large estate, presumably—the narrator did not dwell on such details, but he didn't try to hide them either. She was left on her own with two sons, of whom the older was our companion.

The parents did not belong to any synagogue. At home, the children enjoyed having a Christmas tree hung with silvery tinsel and fairy lights, the echo of a foreign religion in an assimilated family, kept for the amusement of the children, playing happily with their building blocks and tin soldiers. Those tin soldiers were to play another interesting role in the lives of those Jewish children. One day, one of the boys overheard in a grownups' conversation the words: "die Juden."

"Mama, was sind das—Juden?"

"Billige Bleisoldaten, deine sind viel, viel bessere . . . ,"[5] answered the mother, smothering her child's curiosity.

The first years at the Berlin gymnasium, even though before our current turmoil still, taught the children all they had missed about Jews and Jewishness. The school had a very high percentage of pupils from rich, assimilated Jewish families. In their seventh year of school, young boys, out of whose homes any last crumbs of their Jewishness had long been swept clean, were suddenly made to feel Jewish again with all the force of their souls. In those boys, pampered in cleanliness and comfort, separated from their Jewishness as young children

---

3   Germ.: "We sought religious Judaism." (Transl.)

4   A colloquial expression, also used in Polish, for good manners acquired by way of the strict upbringing of children (from German: *Kinder*—"children"; *stube*—"room"). (Transl.)

5   Germ.: "Mom, what are they—Jews?—Cheap lead soldiers, yours are much, much better. . . ." (Transl.)

are protected from things deemed unhealthy, a longing and an urge to learn all there was about the unknown-to-them faith of their forefathers suddenly awoke. "We wanted to return to it while still remaining modern men of culture," our companion told us. So they organized a trip to Poland. They had heard many wonderful stories about Polish ghettoes, which had long disappeared in Germany. I remember how he emphasized at this point that they meant the "religious"—*religiöse*—ghetto. So off they went, visiting all those Mławas and Sochaczews, *heders* and *yeshivas*, talking to old rabbis and their pupils, their peers with whom, however, they could not find a common spiritual language. He told us how they were regarded with suspicion and curiosity. "Dann aber kehrten wir zurück; in dem Ghetto war nicht zu suchen."[6]

This socialist spoke these last words with deep conviction, but also with regret. After their return from Mława, the boys kept together. Later, as students, they became the heart of a kind of club which in German tradition combines elements of tourism and ideology. Its name was, if I remember correctly, Deutsch-Jüdisch Wander-Verein.[7] I certainly remember the "Deutsch-Jüdisch" in the name and how our narrator stressed the primacy of *Deutsch* over *Jüdisch*. In other words—assimilation. But assimilation with a specifically ideological flavor. The assimilation of sons who wanted to be different from their fathers with their Christmas trees and avoidance of any Jewish thought. Within their club, and also beyond it, they conducted a wide campaign among the young. It was a great effort to close the gap which was invisible at the time between *Kinderstube* and *Bleisoldaten*, but which appeared and grew, with them, into an ever bigger crack on the formerly monolithic face of German Jewish assimilation.

To cut a long story short, we went through our rich young man's whole time as a student and his struggle against the growing wave of antisemitism, until at the end of the long, narrowing, and darkening path of assimilation—a great light. Socialism. Marx. At first, those two words seemed to explain it all—the fight against chauvinism and the social implications of labor. The causes of evil and ways of salvation. (He didn't say this clearly, but I felt that it was then that he and his friends began to search for a moral justification for their wealth in view of the widespread poverty of others.) "Mother loved us very much and gave us anything we asked for. But when we needed money for our

---

6   Germ.: "And then we returned; there was nothing to find in the ghetto" (rough translation). (Transl.)

7   Germ.: German Jewish Hiking Club. (Transl.)

organization and the newspaper we wanted to publish, we had to pretend we needed it to pay off debts from our social life."

But Marxism was only a bus stop, both for the two brothers and the whole group. The split, or rather parting of ways in the group, sent them in different directions, some towards communism, others to Zionism. In the spring of 1931, a Zionist group arrived in Palestine. They became the seeds of a German kibbutz.

***

This fundamentally simple story contained, nevertheless, accents or shades which are near impossible to show in full color in such a short summary; it would require the talent of a novelist. When he was relaying his story, and afterwards when we said our goodbyes and took the left turn towards the red roofs of Degania, I had a persistent, if vague, feeling of surprise—so that's how it was!?—and, at the same time, certain equally vague thoughts.

First—just before he met us, the young man must have been alone for the first time in his life. Until then, all his spiritual experiences, all his actions, all his changes and crises, had happened in a group, among his friends. His turn to religion, return to assimilation, the socialism, and Zionism—he had lived through all those processes with other people.

Second—something hung over those young people, my peers from another country and from a different nation, like doctor Judym's[8] Socratic *daimonion*,[9] but in the form of a positive spiritual imperative rather than a dire warning of fate. That imperative threw them literally all over the place until eventually it pulled them apart from their families and homes. It told them to abandon everything with an equanimity which I still sensed in our young companion—leave everything behind without a second thought the way one stops wearing worn-out clothes or stops reading books from which we have learned all they can teach us. That young man was perfectly aware what they meant to their mother, but for them she was first of all the mother of *Bleisoldaten*, the one who readily sponsored their social life but not their political newspaper. They left her with that untrammeled peace of mind which children who were sent off

---

8   Doctor Judym—a central character in Żeromski's *Ludzie Bezdomni*—Homeless People, a
     novel about an enterprising doctor of humble origins, who rebels "against evil and injustice,"
     but is torn between his personal happiness and the success of his mission. (Transl.)
9   Socratic *daimonion*, or *daimon*—an inner attendant spirit; Socrates claimed to have lived his
     life according to the dictates of his *daimon*. (Transl.)

to monasteries used to have, and which, at least for me, always had a sense of impulsive cruelty.

And yet, it was not those two reflections which struck me the hardest. Just then, on the country road from Tel Or to Tiberias, I met, also for the first time in my life, another young man, my peer, from Germany, from the West. I knew and had read a lot about them. I learned that their social class, the same as mine, had not been pauperized by the war in the way mine had been. We were taught that they enjoyed full freedom in all aspects of life. We were used to thinking it was a world without storms or bumpy roads, where one arranges one's life the way one furnishes an apartment with modern comforts and the main focus is on the full realization of life's potential and its enjoyment, including all conceivable liberties and uncomplicated sexual relations.

And now I hear one such a story I used to read about, credible and detailed, with my own ears. And everything I hear is a denial of what I have read. Those young people, those from the front line of the story, and those from the second, the youth of Hitler's Germany—it doesn't really matter which, because for all of them, their life's concern is the exact opposite of what we were told. I remember very well one of my friend's reaction to Bedel's book *L'amour camarade*:[10] he wasn't surprised so much that *à chacun a sa chacune*,[11] but rather by the fact that each student couple had at their disposal at least one car. I can say with complete authority that my companion could easily have had one—perhaps even did—but I could also clearly see that the car and all the rest did not score highly on the stock exchange of his life.

The story of that young Jew erupted like a volcano full of conflicting and destructive forces, but at the same time creative ones. Whatever it might be called—a religious renaissance or atheism, pacifism or militarism, communism or nationalism. In the West, which we wanted to see as sunny-weathered and *plus ça change*, just around the corner from us, something new was brewing, something which a century ago would have been called a "Sturm und Drang Periode."

At the time of our meeting, the young German Jew, a socialist and a Zionist, had all that *Sturm* and *Drang* behind him. He had already found what he was looking for and was no longer interested in exploring other roads. I think, however, that if he had picked up Saint Augustine's confessions he would have recognized in that little book, especially in its opening pages, himself and his fellow travelers—regardless of the years that had passed and the different goals pursued.

---

10   Maurice Bedel (1883–1954)—French novelist and essayist, awarded the Prix Goncourt in 1927 for *Jérôme 60° latitude nord* (Paris: Librairie Gallimard, 1927). (Transl.)

11   Fr.: "every Jack has his Jill." (Transl.)

"A Daemonio Meridiano . . ."

Some nineteen years ago, or even less, Szymon K. would have never thought he would be putting oranges to such improbable and exotic use as planting them. But nineteen years ago it was the year 1914 and Szymon K. was a bookkeeper on one of my cousin's country estates. Every day after breakfast he marched across an already bustling courtyard and set to work in a big, white-washed-clean, and rather empty-looking room, where winters could be cold, often on account of a defective stove, and summers sticky, with flies aplenty even though the village lay in Podolia[1] and not Lithuania. Be it spring or autumn, he could always be seen filling in long columns in all kinds of ledgers with his small, neat handwriting. Everyone at the manor and the farm not only respected him, but simply liked him. Szymon K. was regarded by all as a conscientious, reliable employee and a quiet family man. It well may have been that he would have stayed with the house till the end of his days, certainly for as long as he wanted to, if it weren't for the war and all that followed from it. Somehow our bookkeeper survived the war and found himself in the newly independent Poland. For a few years he worked at a large estate near Przemyśl.[2] In 1924 or 1925, he found his old patron in Warsaw and told him he was going to Palestine.

"How come?" asked my uncle, rather surprised. "And what are you going to do there? Teach Arabs bookkeeping?"

---

1   Podolia (Ukr.), Podole (Pol.)—a historic region in southwestern Ukraine; in prewar Poland, it formed the eastern half of Galicia. (Transl.)

2   Przemyśl—a small historic town in Galicia, now southeastern Poland, close to the Ukrainian border; a town-fortress in the Austro-Hungarian Empire; the birthplace of Rosa Luxemburg. (Transl.)

"In Palestine they give land for colonization," started the bookkeeper, "ten hectares per family. . . ."

"And what, are you going to start ploughing, sowing, and reaping?"

Szymon K. nodded.

"And have you ever held a plough in your hand?"

Szymon K. nodded again, though as the family legend has it—with some hesitation. There was something about the way he answered that made people stop probing him further.

"Well," said my uncle, "may you fare better than here."

And so Szymon K. left. He sent letters saying that potatoes were expensive and oranges frightfully cheap. That life was hard. That already in April it was more humid than Podolia even in July. Then he stopped writing, or they stopped replying. A few years have passed, but a lot has changed. Now someone from the family for whom Szymon worked for so long has come in person to see him in that country, which some ridiculed while others were turning it into a second Promised Land.

* * *

I am sitting with Szymon in front of his house in a small new colony Nahlat Jehuda. The house is just like all the other houses of the private colonists settled here on land provided by the National Fund. Well, not quite like them, for one wall is thicker at the bottom where a step-like whitewashed bench has been formed which in Podolia is called a *przyzba*, except that here it faces north, not south. We sat on it and told each other all we could. I had forgotten what Szymon looked like in the old days, but now the lost memories slowly came back. He must have changed, surely, for he could not have had such a swarthy complexion then, nor such white hair, but he is certainly more energetic than he used to be. He and his wife asked about old friends and acquaintances, receiving the answers with prolonged silences.

Szymon kept returning to one name, time and time again, sighing, "Great shame. . . . What a great shame. . . . " And then he showed me around his *pardes*, full of orange trees with slender trunks and barely a meter tall, but crowned with a blaze of bright-green leaves. Then he took me to see the irrigation system and the rest of his property. The only thing he did not want to show me was his field because, as he said, you won't see a field like we had in Ukraine here. We talked about the economic situation. One can say that Szymon's famous financial acumen was shown at its finest when he invested in that ticket to Jaffa. He is a wealthy man now. The land he paid six pounds a piece for is now worth thirty-eight pounds. The oranges grow well, grapefruit even better. Life is good in Nahlat Jehuda. But it was not always so. . . .

We take our tea under the trees, my hosts are telling me their story. When they arrived here in 1924 it was barren. A copse of trees and dunes. And a well. An old well. The Jewish National Fund settled a dozen families here, gave them land, some stock, and some support. The land remains the property of the Fund, but the settlers can cultivate it as owners; when selling it on, they must conform to the Fund's rules, established to prevent speculation. They are forbidden to hire laborers, so they have worked the land themselves with their children. It's all their sweat. Szymon, when he came here, was forty-nine, including three hard years in the Russian Revolution and the war. Mr. Bookkeeper, who spent his youth and mature years sitting in an office chair hunched over ledgers, Mr. Tillkeeper, who turned up for work at nine, now rose at four to start tilling his red, sandy hill. He planted a few hundred trees here, dug irrigation ditches, reinforced them with concrete walls, built a cowshed, ploughed, sowed, and reaped. A Jew, who for years after his escape from Russia jumped at anything that sounded like a pistol shot, would stand guard every night, rifle in hand. He talks about it with equanimity. He points at a hill from which, during the latest unrest, they fought attacking Arabs. His hands are heavy, look like the two short blades of a hoe. I am sure they looked different when twenty years ago all they were pushing were wooden beads on an abacus.

Szymon K. continues with his story, but I begin to think about something different from a life which sounds just like tens of similar ones I have listened to during my four weeks' crisscrossing the country. It's not what interests me most now. What Szymon is telling me I can hear from any other settler, but what he *can* tell me is what I will not hear from any young *halutz*. Most of the colonists arriving in Palestine are young. All those who have come here to battle—with the desert to make it bloom, with rocks for water, with Arabs for peace—they all brought with them their youthful energy. This man had fifty years on his back when he came here. But I suspect that's not all I could hear from the old bookkeeper. Personally, I remember very little of him from the old days, but the family legend preserved a kind of spiritual portrait of the man. He was not a risk-taker, or a speculator, not a hothead, certainly not an ideologist. He was an ordinary, simple man, except perhaps unusually decent and conscientious. An ideal office clerk. I know for a fact that he could have had his position on the estate near Przemyśl for life. But that is not all. I know people of Szymon's age who lost everything in the Russian Revolution, very wealthy and not-so-wealthy people. But his wealth was hard-earned, acquired through hard work and the use of his vital energies. Others often came out of the revolution utterly broke and broken. Some of them bounced back, true, some miracle workers turned even the most horrific experiences into a success. But how many of them rushed afterwards to the other end of the world to transform themselves into humble colonists, ten-acre farmers? Where did this man's strength come from, not just to survive in brutal circumstances, but to be victorious?

Finally, I share my thoughts with him. I say one sentence only to destroy it with the next, trying to express myself clearly. I don't want to hear another heroic, dead-serious story, but a simple, straightforward one. So I wrap it up with another story.

"There is an old legend, going back to the Middle Ages, told by Catholics. It was recounted mostly among the monks who, saying their Latin prayers, asked God to protect them against the devil and his midday temptations. It went—'A daemonio meridian. . . . .' It was believed that the strongest temptations were visited upon man at midday. And 'midday' didn't just mean the middle of the day, but the middle of life. Even the most placid of men could be taken over by a spirit that would make them throw everything away, change everything. Something might make them get up and go. . . ."

Saying all this, I hope Szymon will pick up his story in the same, if lighter, spirit. That denying the forces of the daemonio meridian he will give me a more pedestrian account of what brought him here, and how. To my surprise, the old bookkeeper quietly affirms:

"Perhaps there is something. . . ."

I am confounded. I didn't expect to find mystics among Zionists. Apparently my confusion shows, for Szymon takes me by the hand and tries to calm me down—no, he didn't really mean it.

And so he tells me:

When he was a young man he'd already heard about Palestine. Long before the war, Jews were leaving Poland. In Petah Tikva, the old colony, there are still three Jews from Cudnów. The owner of one of the hotels in Jerusalem is the son of a Jew from Połonne.[3] Szymon remembers them well. They went, he stayed. He was scared. Too scared, and thought it was not for him. His father gave him a good education, made him a bookkeeper, a quite a comfortable job in those days. Anyway, deep down he felt he was not made for this.

---

3   Cudnów, Połonne—small historic towns which belonged to prepartitioned Poland with a big Jewish population; now in Ukraine. (Transl.)

Szymon confessed that he even gave up a good position when he realized that the man he worked for lived beyond his means. He sought assurance and certainty, to a fault. He invested his money in the best bonds and securities. Never in people. Could there be a more secure investment than a guaranteed bond or a government-backed security?

Szymon waved his hand despondently.

He told me how in a small town he escaped to in 1917 or 1918 he witnessed antisemitic pogroms. He said that he was so stupefied by what he had been through that he wasn't even hiding. He had a non-Jewish name, he didn't look like a Jew, and he survived. But he had not made any effort to do so. As he was was telling me the story—the events of 1918 were fifteen years and thousands of miles away—even now I could hear in his words a quiver of that profound abjection which deadened even the fear of a pogrom in him. He sat now in front of his own house in Palestine still surprised, as if not certain of his own past and history. That such a great state, such a government, and such a safe, quiet country . . . and suddenly . . .

I finally understood. What the old bookkeeper told me was a solution to his riddle that had mystified me all that time.

The Russian Revolution became a revolution in Szymon's life not because it had robbed him of twenty years of savings or nearly killed him. The revolution changed something deeper in him a crossed out a line in a ledger or a depletion of economic resources. The revolution destroyed Szymon's faith in certainty. Even now, in Palestine, in 1933, he was asking himself, and me—could there be anything more certain, safer, more durable than the Russian Empire? He had faith in it the way many others, often Szymon's fellow countrymen, believe in the new Russia. It seems that country still enjoys huge moral credit, even if from time to time it files for bankruptcy.

Returning to Szymon K. His lack of faith in certainty may seem an unusual affliction. Most people who used to believe in the indestructibility of the tsar's ruble converted to the dollar; they changed the object of their faith, but not faith itself. Szymon K., with his total lack of faith in certainty, belongs among the more curious effects in the cabinet of curiosities of the Russian Revolution.

Prerevolutionary Szymon K. had nothing of the speculator about him. He felt instinctively repelled by risk. All he wanted was to be sure, secure. He reckoned that doing his work well would give him all he'd ever wanted from life. He made his calculation with all the deftness and certitude of an accomplished bookkeeper. All wrong.

If Szymon took the job in Przemyśl it was not because he still had any faith in certainty. He was only biding his time before turning his life around. Among people who drew their lessons from the postwar changes, Szymon should be top of the class. His turnaround was complete. For if there is no certainty, there is no room for uncertainty either. When the world belongs to risk-takers, yesterday's bankrupts, and wastrels, one has no option but to follow in their tracks and win it back.

Of course, Szymon put it differently, but that was the gist of it. He was a man of formidable memory and limited fantasy. He remembered well that twenty-nine years before he'd had a choice between two paths—risky Palestine or dependable Russia. He went down one path and came back. Then, without looking for a third, he went down the second. Now that road no longer felt risky. Twenty years after the revolution it didn't feel all that dangerous or difficult. All the forces which had once stifled in him the longing for Eretz Israel now ceased.

I was worried I might miss the last bus to Jaffa and had to take my leave. Once more, Szymon asked me to tell him the legend about the midday devil. At that moment, Palestine and all her problems fell away. Shaking each other hands we knew we were saying good bye for the last time, and not just to each other as men, but to the whole old world—people, their work, and customs— irrevocably lost.

31

Roads

Along mountain range protects Jerusalem from the sea. It doesn't seem to have done good job, for all along it are the ruins of old fortresses and castles, which no one knows now whether they were built by the Crusaders or the Saracens. Seen from the highest hilltop they look like a random group of huge turtle shells strewn all over the place. They are grayish brown, deathly pale. Winding through it, like a stream that never dries even in the greatest heat, runs a glistening ribbon of a road. That is what it is like across the whole of Palestine. I have a feeling that if we set off early enough in a good car, by the evening we would have crisscrossed this country in all directions, visiting Jerusalem, Jericho, the Dead Sea, Bethlehem, Hebron, Jaffa, and Tel Aviv, form there moving north to Nahalal and Afula to Haifa, and from Haifa further up to Nazareth and Tiberias. The sophisticated tourist admires the quality of Palestinian tarmac; all travelers praise the British administration and its roadbuilding program. At which point the modest Brits bow and acknowledge that—yes, we can confirm that indeed our roads are fairly good and that for all the major routes here we used the same quality of tarmac as on Welsh and Scottish roads.

But the British administration is mistaken. The tarmac on the roads to Jerusalem and Haifa (where one stretch is particularly bad, apparently purposefully so to stop the car traffic completely outrunning the railways), that tarmac is altogether different from that covering Scottish and Welsh roads, or for that matter, all other roads in the rest of the world.

＊

Fourteen years ago, there were none of the roads that cover Palestine today. Eleven years ago, there may have been a sign that there would be some roads built for the military. The Ottoman administration left Palestine a road system from the time of Suleiman or even Richard the Lionheart. The British plans got stuck on one insurmountable problem—the lack of a workforce. Arab laziness blended naturally with the first "no cooperation" protests. At the same time, professional opinion was that roadbuilding in Palestine was simply beyond the ability of the white man, not to mention the rules which prohibited the white man from roadbuilding in colored countries. Well, the first claim perhaps may have some truth in it. The future road system had to be cut through mountains sometimes as high as 1,000 meters above sea level. On some days, even the Thomas Cook agency stops their tours going through these parts, as the heat radiating from the rocks makes the journey unbearable, even in a luxurious air-conditioned coach with shaded windows. What is really dangerous are the plummeting temperatures. They come out of nowhere—from behind a rock's edge or a mountain slope, an icy blast suddenly strikes, streams of cold air rising from deep valleys. Nights here are not cold, they are freezing cold. Then there is general lack of water and threat of malaria, which only ten years ago accounted for thirty to sixty percent of deaths in Palestine.

Roadbuilding turned out to be an attractive work proposition for young Jews. Everyone remembers the universal doubt with which we all greeted the Jewish rush into farming. We did not believe in Jews' aptitude for farming, nor in the rush itself. We did not believe they would bother with the land. Meanwhile, they started working on the roads. It was not a gesture towards the British, but a point of political importance for the Zionists. Jews were acutely aware by then that the Arab anti-road attitude was a defense against the return of Israel; it was a way of making possible an attack while hindering quick relief from the towns. The Jews simply followed the Roman tactic of fettering a conquered province with a chain of hard beaten roads.

Most of the new roads were built in six years. That period passed into Palestinian history as the "time of crisis." For many reasons. First of all, the postwar poverty in middle and eastern Europe, combined with the closing of the United States to new immigration, rerouted the flow of the Jewish immigration to Palestine. And that flow brought not just the Zionist idealist, but mostly the impoverished masses. At that time, the rich Jewish colonists tended to hire local Arab workers as they were cheaper and less demanding. That narrowed successful colonization to the wealthier among the new arrivals. Subsequently, those two factors caused the re-emigration of Jews. What was worse, the Jews who returned to the Diaspora countries brought back with them their disappointment and lack of faith in the Palestinian project. The whole Zionist idea wobbled. Everyone was bashing it with anything that came to hand, from all sides—the communists, the chauvinists, under the banner of the Internationale and in the name of the nations.

I didn't see Palestine at that time, the time of roadbuilding. By now the roadbuilders have come down into to the valleys, they plant vines and oranges. I can't think my way into the mind of a roadbuilder, but can't help thinking that, as far as I can tell, if the Palestine idea managed to survive that crisis it was thanks to the roadbuilding. The heat, the cold and the backbreaking labor—those were not the largest obstacles for the *halutzim*. Those people knew what was happening in the valleys. They knew that many of those who fled Palestine were people who found too much work and too little profit here and who were aware of the speculations of the rich colonists. They knew too that the immigration flow out of the Diaspora had been reduced to a trickle and could even dry up completely. That they themselves, the best colonist material, were thinning out with every month of work, with every mile of road.

In such circumstances, one would expect only one reaction, similar to the one felt by a frontline soldier who knows he has only chaos and defeatism behind his back. Palestine knew the story of Saint Jean d'Acre, the last stronghold of the Crusaders, which fell to Islam not as a result of a two-year siege, but only when the defenders realized that back in Europe the fate of the Holy Land was no longer of interest to anyone.

In 1926, when the influx of migration dropped to the minimum, it was women who came forward and took the returnees places on the frontline. After a few months, there were hundreds of them working. This was their reaction to the crisis. But from then on, the returning immigrants started spreading a different story about Palestine—about the roads, the *halutzim*, and the girls. Against the background of the blackest hopelessness in Brudno and Nalewki,[1] that story painted a different, previously unseen image of the new Jew. Slowly, that new, inexplicable Jew, his back bent over the road, grew and overshadowed everything else in Palestine, its whole history, even the Wailing Wall. The presence of that Jew in Eretz became the most pressing matter. Palestine and the dream of a better life turned into a picture of backbreaking, heroic labor.

---

1   Brudno and Nalewki—Jewish districts of Warsaw before World War II. (Transl.)

And together with that image—Palestine dawned anew. Now, each returning immigrant became, without any effort on his part, a herald of the cause that he had just deserted. Perhaps he still had a demoralizing effect on some people, but to others he was a walking advertisement. The crisis was over.

***

"Breaking stones on the road" is the proverbial hardest of all hard work. But it was not the difficulty of it or the really harsh conditions that were the biggest obstacle. One had to have a really huge stock of enthusiasm and a simple, unbreakable faith in the project of hacking the road out of the rock, while being aware one may be hacking it out for the British, the Arabs, and American tourists—but not for the future Eretz Israel. This thought must have weighed down like lead on the arm every time it raised the hammer, hampering the power of each strike. The monotonous, tedious work must have grown even slower and more tedious, even more unbearable. The clang of the hammers must have echoed with the questions—What for? For whom? Why?

Just then, at some point on the Tiberias-Nazareth road, a new worker turned up. He was an Oxford student, the son of the British high commissioner. A Jew with a rather loose connection to the traditions of his native land, one Erwin Samuel. The *halutzim* were pointing at the rose-cheeked and a portly little son of an English "sir"; they even made up a mocking song—"Erwin, Erwin, this road is not a tennis court,"—and told him not to practice volleys and smashes. It took him time to earn the respect of the *halutzim*. He is now the governor of Nazareth County. Great Britain has many governors in her colonies, but the colonial history of the empire does not know a case in which the son of the king's appointee broke stones on the road. White British officials are not allowed to frequent the homes of the local population. Even if the "local population" boasts ancestry going back to the prophets. Yet the British allowed the son of the king's deputy to hack out roads and pour tarmac in front of the "colored population." For the British, it was not a "policy" or a "fancy," but something closer to a salute.

32

The Threat of Soviet Cannons

A few days before my departure for Syria, I witnessed a strange event. At dawn, I left on a bus but not necessarily for one of the colonies. Tel Aviv was only just beginning to wake up, I was accompanied by workers traveling to work. Suddenly they all jumped up and rushed to the windows. Somewhere between Tel Aviv and Jaffa, on a bend in the road, three policemen were pulling a banner down from a telegraph pole. The banner was red, and in this country, where all public notices are bi- or even trilingual, this one was written only in one language: Arabic.

What struck me was the vocal hostility with which my fellow travelers, the workers, greeted the sight. Soon I received a full and fully satisfying explanation: the communist banner read: "Down with Jewish-British Imperialism!"

***

If you find a Jewish communist—not a "political" communist, in the sense of being on the payroll of USSR—but a communist-idealist, a man who, based on his own thinking, has come to the conclusion that communism is a both higher and better form of social system, and if that Jew, instead of emigrating to communist Russia comes to Palestine to live in a kibbutz, then soon after arriving his jaw will hit the floor: he will learn that this Palestinian socialist movement, the kibbutz movement, is most aggressively fought against by . . . communists. He will learn that the emissaries of the USSR are trying to agitate the Arab masses against the Jews and that they are as good at it as the most rabid nationalists. Inasmuch as it is hard to believe that there could be a direct connection between Grand Mufti El Hussain, the leader of Arab nationalism, and the communists, it seems pretty obvious that such a cooperation must de facto be taking place, at least between the minor officials of both organizations. And it is not the private Jewish colonists who are the main target of their attacks. On the contrary: the form of colonization which the communist emissaries attack most strongly is the communist form—of the *kibbutzim*. And the one which is attacked only sparingly is the private colony.

At first, our communist cannot believe this is so. But when he has more than enough evidence for it, he gets confused. How come? After all, it is the Jewish immigration and its capital that have accelerated this country's social progress and economic development, dragging it from feudalism to capitalism, which according to Marx is the last stop before arriving at communism. After all, it was Jewish immigrants who brought their share of European rationalism and anticlericalism here, also a significant contribution in a country like this. The formation of a proletarian class here can also be dated to the time of their arrival and it is also they who organize Arab workers, even fight for their rights, spread, and cultivate their class awareness. And it was they, after all, who created those economic communes which function so well here. Comparing a kibbutz with the Arab villages surrounding it is the best propaganda for its advanced form of economy. The Jewish contribution to the revolutionary movements in Europe, especially to communism, is so great that this alone should—one would think—be enough to warrant, if not sympathy, at least a neutral attitude towards their work. And yet, the communists attack Jewish settlements in Palestine more ferociously than Arab nationalists and even more systematically.

So, how do we normally see Soviet Russia? It seems that our view of Russia was shaped, even if unconsciously, by the "Russian Whites," the has-beens sitting now in the Berlins and Parises, who have been saying for years: "Russia is no more; Russia, our motherland, fell because of an unfortunate set of events into the hands of an international thieving band, a mafia, which took it over, and which for years has been sacrificing Russia's best interest to its own, international goals." Our view of Russia, then, is the view of the old White Guard. Russia, they think, is just a tool in the hands of communists in their geopolitical game. Russia is the place where they try to implement their non-Russian goals.

But in the Middle East it looks different.

Here, the Anglo-Russian rivalry is not just a journalistic phrase, a banner in a demonstration, the spur to coffeehouse disputations. It is reality. Everyone here knows that any move, not just by a country such as Afghanistan or Iran, but by any local chief on the Euphrates or near Medina, is made under the influence of one of the two empires locked in a battle to control ever greater parts of the world. The Anglo-Russian battle in Europe, its military interventions and anti-Soviet crusade—this is a spent force. Our great European industry is no enemy of five-year planning, but is its obsequious *Hoflieferant*.[1] But here, in Asia, things are different. Everyone here knows that a confrontation will take place, that now the game is less suspended than continued now, but with all the cards kept close to one's chest. India, Persia, Afghanistan, all the khanates and emirates, all the tribes from the largest to the smallest, nations and clans one doesn't even know exist—all are pieces on the chessboard in the game between Ivan and John. Everyone knows it and everyone has placed his bets. In this game, as is often the case in all long-drawn-out and close battles, the stakes seem to have been long forgotten, only sheer fighting instinct spurs it on. And in such a game any ally is good.

The fact is that the Soviets cannot count on any communist enthusiasts in Asia. People would have to be educated to comprehend the teachings of communism first there. The work of "awakening class consciousness" in societies often stuck in the Middle Ages is too slow for the dynamic Kremlin. In Asia, communism has only one way forward: to win the masses with noncommunist slogans, catchy slogans which will be readily understood by the simplest and most backward Bedouins and Afghans. Typically, these are nationalistic slogans or, rather, anti-European ones. And for allies one has to make do with all kinds of Pan-Arabism or Pan-Islamism—it does not matter that at their helm stand not just rich magnates, but also religious leaders. For now (and it is a rather long-lasting "now") this matter is of minute importance for the communists. The only important consideration is that they are anti-British. In other words: *poputchiki*—fellow travelers. I think it was the SRs (the Russian Social Revolutionaries)[2] who accused the Bolsheviks of gaining power by stealing their slogan about universal agrarian reform, which they had no intention of ever putting into practice anyway, but thanks to which they won the overwhelming support of the Russian peasantry. Perhaps one day, Arab nationalists will be accusing Bolsheviks from their exile, and equally futilely, that they stoles their slogans and only thanks to this have they achieved power. Perhaps. For now, the final confrontation is some way off. For now they are only fellow travelers.

---

1   Royal Seal of Approval (Germ.). (Transl.)
2   SR, Social Revolutionary Party—a major political party in prerevolutionary Russia; a rival of the Bolshevik Party; after the October Revolution, its members were persecuted and destroyed by the victorious Bolsheviks. (Transl.)

As I said, Jews are the target of the strongest attacks from Arab nationalists, which however have proved utterly ineffective. The founding of the Jewish "home" in Palestine, the Jewish settlement program and its future development, in Arab minds all that is closely linked with the arrival of the British, the British occupation, and the continued presence of the British on the Jordan. A classic, ideal argument for anti-British agitation is thus the "Jewish question"!

Having once stepped on this path, communists have to press on. They have to turn first against Jewish collective colonization, collective and not private. Why? It's simple. Collective colonization is that form which is most hated by the Arabs. In private colonies, Arabs very often find work; private colonization brings into the country fewer Jews and more capital; with private colonization the population growth is smaller than in the *kibbutzim*. It will be easier to remove a Jewish owner from the land one day than a whole Jewish village.

This is the reasons why collective colonization is, and must be, the most reviled by the Arab nationalists. The communists, having taken up the muftis and effendis for allies, and concluded that stirring up nationalism will accelerate the confrontation and so bring forward the day of an open class conflict, logically had to follow a path which, paradoxically, brought them into conflict with . . . another sort of communism.

This is the kind of politics that will make any follower of Marx, though not one familiar with the practices of Soviet politics, protest vigorously. These people do not understand how fellow traveling works; all they see is that in their struggle against the British, the atheist proletarian state has joined the clerics and capitalists, the reactionary far right. These people do not see that on the Soviets' road into Asia lies the destruction of Zionist Palestine, the kibbutz, and the *moshav*, of colonies which have given Jews shelter and where they are happy. The more sympathetic these people were towards the USSR, the more hostile they are to it now. For apart from seeing communism as their national enemy, they also see it has having betrayed a great idea, the idea they were also devoted to. This alliance with muftis and effendis discredits communism more than any financial malversation by the communists in Baranowicze or Suwałki.[3]

Three years ago, a distinguished communist, an ethnic Tartar and an envoy to one of the eastern courts, went on the traditional Muslim pilgrimage to Mecca. Our press made fun of the officially godless official who "took his

---

3 Baranowicze, Suwałki—small towns in prewar Poland with large Jewish populations; Baranowicze is now in Belarus; Suwałki is in northeastern Poland. (Transl.)

prayers in Kaaba and visited the tomb of the prophet," providing all the sordid details of how many times the "Red pilgrim" had to bow and kneel piously. It was funny to us. But it has to be said that, while we do not really care if communism enters dubious compromises, for an idealist, though perhaps not for a Soviet communist, this news must have been quite distasteful.

Yet, in Asia such things happen every day. The use of "fellow travelers" can be quite fruitful. Still, its implementation in Asia does more harm than good. When looking out for fellow travelers during the Russian Revolution, the sheer speed of changes justified "departing from the party line," while other, more dramatic, events soon eclipsed the bad impression of any such moral somersault. The Middle East is relatively stable and the tempo of transformation rather slow. There, a risky political deal does not bring the kind of quick and rewarding results seen in Russia in 1917–1923. And so the method is harder to defend in the eyes of a true communist.

Seen from Europe, Russia is communist Russia, a Russia whose interests are subservient to Marxist doctrine. But Russia seen from Asia, the Middle East, is different. It's a country where the state, its political machinery, has absorbed Marxist teaching and uses it for its own advantage; it is a tool Russia is not loath to use, alongside other tools. During my travels here I heard a very interesting comparison—communism is Russia's new Orthodoxy. It was here in the Turkish Orient that Russia spent long years and many millions to propagate its Orthodox religion, with a clear political end in mind. Orthodoxy was fully controlled by the imperialist patriarchy, it was a tool of the Russian national interest, its *raison d'état*. And it was still its official, overriding doctrine. Today, communism has taken its place in all those contexts. Yet the Russian political goal in Asia remains the same—to destroy British influence. Perhaps the inner reasons for it have changed, but the goal is the same, and everyone can see that. Arab nationalism here is an even better tool than communism. The theory of stirring up a national revolution in order to convert it into a class revolution has been put to work. These are the broad tactical lines of attack. Of these broad lines a Jewish colonist sees and understands only one thing—that communism, Russia, is against Jewish settlement in Palestine. Never mind why, the main thing for him is that it is against.

The paradoxes of Soviet politics in Asia require decoding. One thing, however, does not need much explaining, namely that the Arab danger, whatever form it may take, pales in comparison with the danger to the Jewish project of a Soviet victory in Asia. This would be mean its end in Palestine.

The main force waging war against the rebuilding of the State of Israel—relentless, constant, now and in the future—is Soviet Russia. It reckons that it is better to win over millions of Arabs than 200,000 Palestinian Jews. What it does not seem to be reckoning with is that Palestine is not just being rebuilt by the Jews who are already here. It is being rebuilt by all the Jews in the world, by millions. For those Jewish masses, this project today is the most important of all, it matters to them as much as the idea of regaining independence did to the Poles. Whoever stands in their way becomes their enemy, irrespective of past bonds of friendship. Jewry has been a faithful supporter of all the revolutionary movements of the past and present century. Assimilated Jewry has always stood on the revolutionary side of the barricades. Zionist Jewry has crossed into a field of fire and has found itself exposed to attack from revolutionary Russia. And so it has had to open a new frontline.

One of the most important achievements of Zionist Palestine is giving this great, historically rich nation a new political direction. It may be the beginning of a portentous change, fraught with consequences that will be felt not just in the Middle East, but everywhere where Jews live in the world. Until recently, the only star that shone on the abject poverty of the ghetto was the red star of communism. When the six-pointed Zionist star of the national renaissance began to rise next to it, no one would have expected it was rising to fight the red star for the heart of its nation. This struggle will be titanic and today it is only beginning. However, it has already brought Jewry onto a path it has not trodden for millennia. The Palestinian project is not threatened by Arab daggers, but by Soviet cannons.

Afterword

Coming to the end of my observations, I find it extremely difficult to give the reader something like a comprehensive synthesis of my Palestinian impressions. I travelled the length and breadth of the land, talked to a host of people, both ordinary individuals and eminent people, the leaders of communities. I experienced the full spectrum of emotions, many of them powerful. And yet—and it is not the author's false modesty speaking now—I cannot find for them the words they deserve.

It would be difficult to meet anyone more detached from the life of the Jewish community than the author. Coming from a landowning family of the old Polish eastern borderland (now "cordoned off" behind the Soviet border), apart from occasional trading relationships we had no connections with Jews. Even among our remotest family connections I cannot find a Jewish link, even with an assimilated Jew. I am deeply attached to my religion in which the role of Jews has not always been seen in a favorable light and among whose clerics antisemitic attitudes are strong to this day. My traditional upbringing in a country manor instilled in me many gentile, even feudal, customs which I knew to be foreign, if not hostile, to Jews, yet which I accepted as "my own." All this did not make me close to Jewish culture, nor did it teach me to understand it.

In my Ukrainian childhood I saw the Jewish pogroms of 1919. My university years were during a time when the autumn recruitment campaigns for nationalistic student fraternities traditionally started with large crowds rounding upon terrified Jewish individuals. Whoever thinks this is just the high jinks of hotheaded youth—as our newspapers claim—let him visit our universities during the next autumn campaign. I have. And despite their most learned and most authoritative justifications—I do not believe them. I do not believe it is either the right way to solve the "Jewish problem" in Poland or that it is a good exercise for the young in "holy service to the nation."

All this made me feel that I was facing an open wound. A basic moral feeling did not allow me not to condemn it at the time. My civic instinct told me that finding a solution to the "Jewish problem" in Poland was badly needed, necessary even. I came to the conclusion that, first of all, one needs to understand this issue and that in turn meant for me to listen to the "other side."

When a young Jew, an academic activist with whom I had become friends, talked to me about Palestine, like most Poles I listened to him skeptically at first. But the more often I spoke about it with other Jews the more convinced I became that there was more to this than we Poles realized; that this Palestine of theirs—whether Jews were emigrating there or not—was slowly, but surely, emerging into the foreground of their thinking. It was something I acknowledged, but whose consequences I did not quite fathom. So a few years later I decided to see it for myself.

The significance of Palestine for "the Jewish problem" rests, it seems to me, on two things: firstly—Jewish emigration, which, if it succeeds in overcoming the British who ruthlessly limit all immigration there, may play a decisive role. Secondly, Palestine has already become the spiritual capital of the world's Jewry, similar to the role of Cracow for the Poles before 1914. What is happening in Palestine now has an immediate resonance throughout the Jewish Diaspora in Western Europe, America, and in Poland. The changes that are taking place there have a direct bearing both on world politics and on the Jewish mindset. This in turn affects Polish Jewish relations back at home and this influence, to my mind, is wholly positive.

The Jews in Poland have often been accused of supporting communism, that communism which for us means not only a social revolution but also losing two-thirds of Poland's territories—the east to Russia, Pomerania and Silesia to Germany—at least according to the program of the communist parties in Poland, which apparently have vocal supporters among their Jewish activists. Communism as an idea cannot be defeated by police measures; it can only be defeated by another idea. It has happened without our involvement, but it seems that Zionism is exactly this, making steady and irrevocable advances among the Jews at the cost of communism, and fighting it. Hitlerism is destroying German Jews in a terrible way, hounding and torturing them, but Russian communism has already annihilated the existence of one of the largest Jewish centers in the world. It has cut it off from the rest of the Jewish world and is now melting it down in the crucible of its "national policies." The Soviets have turned out to be the most dangerous enemy of the Jews. The threat of communism is too important from the point of view of our national interests for this development to be ignored.

Zionism also fights against the assimilation of the Jews, tries to prevent its progress. I have nothing against the assimilation of individuals, the kind that has given us people like Julian Klaczko.[1] But probably no one in Poland, with the possible exception of the socialists, wishes for the assimilation of the Jewish masses. Assimilation is not in the Jewish national interest either and the most effective dam against Jewish assimilation is the work of Zionists.

Zionism consistently works to halt assimilation, so that instead of continual seepage from the Jewish community for the benefit of Polish society, Jewry can constitute itself as an independent organism, primarily political and national, not just religious. I could risk a comparison, if only a partial one—a return to the ghetto: to the kind of community which is concerned above all with its own life and its own quarrels and one with whom our cohabitation will not continuously strain national unity with unresolvable conflicts.

I do not feel ready, nor is it my place, to offer or even investigate a solution to the "Jewish problem" in Poland. However, it seems to me that in our discussions about this issue everybody ignores the work of the Zionist movement and what it has achieved in Palestine. And yet, this movement is having a deeper and broader influence on the three-million-strong group of citizens of our country every day, and the reconstruction of Eretz Israel—Palestine—is a fact.

***

Things Jewish have been foreign to me, as foreign as those same things are close to my Jewish compatriots. Nevertheless, there are passages in this book that are written with a genuine enthusiasm that, in the eyes of the reader, may perhaps undermine the coolly detached character which a true reporter should possess; and they may see me as tendentious or unduly sympathetic. Such a tendency is alien to me, like the fellow Poles of my generation who cannot be said to be filled with warm feelings for the Jewish cause. There are things in this world that simply spark enthusiasm, not just things foreign, but things that are profoundly different.

This land in which I travelled revealed itself to me as an equal among its great historic neighbors. Standing before the pyramids of Egypt, I was struck by

---

1   Julian Klaczko (1825–1906)—born Jehuda Lejb; a popular and influential author, journalist, historian, and politician; a prime example of successful assimilation into Polish culture. (Transl.)

the assiduousness with which those civilizations tried to preserve something of themselves for the future. Tens of centuries before Horace's "Non omnis moriar . . . magnaque pars mei vitabit Libitina. . . ."[2] The fear of death in all-powerful Egypt found its expression in the royal mausoleums, the tombs of statesmen, priests, and sages of their culture, the wonders of the word. Yet what are these compared with the instinct of the Israelites, which is harder than stones, an instinct rooted and cultivated by their laws of religion, custom, and community; by their poetry, and the fullness of a spiritual life which has managed to preserve the whole nation better than the Egyptians preserved the mummies of their pharaohs, to protect it against external factors better than the thickest blocks of granite?

And not just compared to Egypt, but also to Hellas—how small is Judea! Remember Titus Quinctius, Consul Flamininus? A Roman magnate, a statesman, and a general who ended Macedonian hegemony in Greece. His legions marching into Athens were commanded by sons of Rome who also spoke the melodious tongue of Xenophon and Plato on whose writings they had been raised. This clearly had a large influence on them. From a loge in the Olympic stadium in Athens, the Roman consul proclaimed the resurrection of an independent Greece. But that independence was just an empty word which was not—and could not be—filled with any meaningful content. Resurrected Hellas turned out to be a delusion, despite Homer, despite Phidias.

These is, however, a parallel between this action of Hellenized Rome and its political heir in today's world—the British Empire. Field Marshall Allenby's forces which marched into the Holy Land were raised on the Bible and the Old Testament, so important to Protestants. All Allenby's orders exuded that biblical spirit, as did all the accounts of his exploits in the press. When Great Britain proclaimed the resurrection of Judea, it too was a historical act reminiscent of the gesture of that Roman consul. But here the analogies end. The resurrection of Hellas failed barely a couple of centuries after the Battle of Chaeronea.[3] Just as Egypt survived only in its physical monuments, so has Hellenic Greece only in the hexameters of the *Iliad*. Yet eighteen centuries of Judea's lethargy did not end in death. Of those three ancient civilizations, this one has salvaged the

---

2   Lines from Horace's Ode 3.30: "I shall not wholly die . . . and a great part of me will avoid the grave . . ." (Latin). (Transl.)

3   The Battle of Chaeronea—regarded as one of the most decisive battles of the ancient world, fought between Philip of Macedon and a coalition of Greek states in 338 BC, which ended the independence of Greek *poleis*. (Transl.)

most—the nation. Balfour's declaration has avoided the fate of Flamininus's proclamation. A fate that seemed probable, nay, certain.

This country's past has always been balanced precariously between two extremes, so beautifully expressed in the Oriental richness of the ancient tongue of the prophets: Palestine has either been a land flowing with milk and honey or one where no stone has been left standing upon stone; today, it is again going through a milk and honey phase. From out of the historical frame of its past, there emerged something still greater and very different from it—the era of Christianity. But apart from the birth of Christianity, Palestine has twice influenced the course of human history—first with its Hebrew history, then with the history of Crusades. In both cases, what happened in this small and seemingly insignificant country had a worldwide resonance. I have a feeling that one day soon the consequences of the Zionist renaissance will rank in the same order of magnitude as Palestine's previous two entries into world history.

Appendix:
Ksawery Pruszyński's
Speeches to the UN

As chair of Subcommittee One, one of the two set up by the Ad Hoc Committee on the Question of Palestine in October 1947, Pruszyński gave two important speeches. Unfortunately, neither of these speeches have been archived in any official records of the UN or the Polish Foreign Office and their full original texts remained unknown to the public, as well as historians, for over seventy years.

The first speech was delivered on November 25, 1948 at the closing session of the Ad Hoc Committee on the Palestinian Question, when the committee delivered its final report. In his speech, Pruszyński addressed questions and issues raised by the other members of the committee, explaining the difficulties involved in arriving at the final version of the proposal and defending it as the only possible, if uneasy, compromise. The text presented here is a faithful transcription of Pruszyński's handwritten note, preserving his original style, just as he delivered it. The manuscript was only discovered in December 2019, found in the private archive of Mieczysław Pruszyński (1910–2005). It is the first publication of the English original in extenso.

The second speech was delivered on November 29 in Lake Success when the proposal contained in the report of Subcommittee One was put to the vote before the General Assembly as Resolution 181. The text presented here is an extract from that speech prepared by the author for publication in the Polish-language Zionist paper *Opinia* in 1948.[1] It appeared there as "Polska i Erec" (Poland and the Land of Israel). The speech was reprinted in 1990 as part of

---

1   "Polska i Erec" (Poland and the Land of Israel), *Opinia* (Łódź; Tel-Aviv), no. 28 (1948).

Pruszyński's collected journalism.[2] Here it is published for the first time in English (in a translation of the Polish translation); the full text of the original speech is yet to be found.

—Wiesiek Powaga

---

2   *Publicystyka*, vol. 2, *1940–1948: Powrót do Soplicowa*, ed. Gotfryd Ryka and Janusz Roszko (Warszawa: Państwowy Instytut Wydawniczy, 1990), 402–405.

Mr. President,[3]

I would like to try, with your most kind permission to proceed to a summing up of what has been said during these last three days, when, as we all remember, two different reports and two different draft resolutions were presented to this committee. You have both in front of you, and you have already heard during that debate, different views and different opinions. Listening to them all, I realised the very important difference existing between the draft resolutions as presented by the Subcommittee No. 2 and that one which has been presented by the Subcommittee No. 1 of which I had the most unexpected and most certainly undeserved honour to be the acting chairman. That very important difference is that the members of Subcommittee No. 2, or, speaking otherwise, of the Arabic Subcommittee, are all feeling extremely enthusiastic and extremely sure that their project, elaborated during a couple of days, is a perfect and excellent work, done easily and promptly.

We of the Subcommittee No. 1, or, with other words, the Subcommittee of Partition, have never congratulated ourselves for our work. It took us several weeks of time, during which we were working hard, as the honourable representative of Syria has already pointed out. Twice we had to apologise before you, Mr. Chairman, and before this illustrious assembly for the slowness and delay of our work. When coming here, we presented you with a solution about which we were far from being enthusiastic. Quite on the contrary. We all pointed out and stressed the difficulties, the complications even the many dangers of our own plan. We never denied that we presented you with a solution complicated because the situation, the reality of the land we were concerned with is difficult, troubled, complicated and divided. The plan of Subcommittee No. 2, that of our distinguished concurrents is easy and straight. That which is the product of wishful thinking, of what we would like to see, not what actually exists, is always extremely easy, and childishly straight.

It has been said, and I think that the honourable delegate of Syria has said it, that just work is easy and simple while a work which is not just is—as ours was—hard and long.

I don't think that this opinion is justified. The map, as presented by Subcommittee No. 2 is clear and simple. There is no frontier on it. Strangely enough, it looks just like that map of the past, that map of the gloomy and dark

---

3   Speech by Ksawery Pruszyński, Polish delegate and chairman of Subcommittee One of the United Nations' Ad Hoc Committee on the Question of Palestine, delivered in Lake Success at the closing session of the Ad Hoc Committee on November 25, 1947.

days of the Ottoman Empire. Our map, the map of Palestine, as presented by the Subcommittee No. 1, the Subcommittee of Partition is complicated and divided. We know it. We apologise for it. But, if we apologise for it, somebody could ask—why have you prepared something so complicated and divided? Mr. Chairman, I have a straight reply on that question. Our plan is difficult, our map is complicated, because the situation in Palestine is so difficult and so complicated.

When working on a plan we had to submit to this most distinguished assembly that we were not relying only on our own knowledge and work. We have adopted as a basis of our work the report, prepared by a commission sent long before to Palestine by the United Nations. That commission spent many months at work. We took into consideration the reports and observations of many previous commissions, which at some earlier or later stage have proceeded us in our study of that very complicated situation in a particularly endangered country. And we found, what was so admirably expressed by the honourable representative of China, and what is unfortunately not understood enough by our Arabian colleagues, that really the Palestinian case is a unique one. It can't be compared to that of Korea, or modern Greece or to any other. Perhaps just for that reason a purely legalistic and strictly juridical argumentation will never size up quite completely the whole of that question. Yes, there is some unique thing in that small part of land, which is the country of the Bible, the most widely read book of our world, the birth place of three great religions, the country of Christ. There is something quite unique, even in our sad world, to the story of that never too numerous nation which, after having contributed more than any other to the basis of our civilisation, became an eternal errant throughout a steadily hostile world. There is something unique in the way this great nation, the Jewish one, made a religion of their longing for their lost home. There is something unique in that revival, after two thousand years, of a nation. You can call it dreams, you can call it phantasy, you can call it lack of reality. You can and you may call it as you like. You may justly say that after two thousand years all historical rights are long extinct. . . . But in spite of how you will call what is in modern times the revival of the Jews as a nation—it is still a fact. It is a fact that from some decades, people of Jewish religion living in Vienna, in the Balkans, in Germany, in Warsaw, in Jewish quarters of London or Paris or Casablanca or Odessa or elsewhere, felt that their life is not where they have been born and where their fathers and forefathers were born and died, but in a country quite distant and even exotic for them. They came to Palestine being or not being persecuted, they came despite the fact that London, or Paris, or New York or other countries beyond the ocean represented to them better, materially better, possibilities. They came to a poor, remote, neglected country, to work hard, yes, I may say, very hard, as hard as never any white man has worked in what is called colonial lands. People who have been said to be completely strange to any physical work, and most particularly to any agricultural one, people who during centuries presented us with bankers, usurers, Shylocks, went now in a sandy desert and transformed that sandy desert into a nourishing orchard, came into what had been marshes infested by malaria and changed it into fields.

Mr. Chairman, honourable Delegates, please, look at that map you have in front of you. Look at this complicated difficult map. This map with corridors, with enclaves, with so-called points of intersection. Why this map [is] so complicated? This map is so complicated just because the Jews, when settling, came to what have been the worst land. They came to those barren, desolated sand hills along the coast from Haifa to Jaffa, where there was nothing but sand and where now is nothing but an orchard. They came to that long valley, linking Haifa with the Jordan, where once more there was nothing but marshes and malaria. They left the whole hilly land, settled, inhabited and cultivated by the Arabs—to the Arabs. Always in history, invaders took the best land for themselves. The Jews took what was the worst, they paid for it. Not only with money, but with sweat, tears and blood they paid many times its value.

This map, gentlemen, like the report of the Subcommittee No. 1, like all the work of that Subcommittee No. 1 represents a compromise. Its boundary line goes between what the Arabs possessed from centuries and what the Jews acquired by an effort as great as not many nations have ever effectuated. Once more, an effort quite unique.

Yes, Mr. Chairman, we are very far from proposing you a solution which we would call easy or simple or straight. What we are proposing is—as the representative of Canada said—a best possible solution in a difficult, particularly difficult, situation. There was not a single word by which we ever tried to diminish the danger of the question, nor the responsibilities of the UN. But just because it is a *cas unique*, just because it is danger, just because it is difficult, just because responsibility is involved, we felt and we feel that it is the task, the duty—yes, the duty of the United Nations—to deal with this situation. We feel, that in that case we need a very strong cooperation of all of us. Of the Mandatory Power, of all the United Nations, of the Palestinian population.

I have heard many angry words on the part of the Arab delegations. I am not at all surprised. I am not at all angry for it. I am just sorry for two things.

First, that a political partition of Palestine was inevitable, secondly, that it could not be proceeded to in a better mutual spirit. You all remember that the Arabs have refused all participation in the work of the United Nations Special Committee on Palestine, that the last chance of conciliation, initiated by you Mr. Chairman, was similarly and most unfortunately lost. One of the first steps of the Subcommittee No. l was to invite to its meetings a representative of the Arab High Committee. Once more they refused. I can very frankly assure you of one thing. During all our dealings we had no bad feelings against the Arabs. I had just the best feelings for them. They are a proud race, they are a valiant race, and perhaps similarly to the Poles, they were in the last two hundred years at least an unhappy race. I think I may say, that the foreign policy of my country, Poland, has supported in the past and will support in the future all the justifiable claims of Arabic nations. We voted for the introduction to the UN of several Arabic States, although they we were not always completely sure they were complying quite exactly to all the required conditions.

We, Polish people, have special reasons to promote the State of Israel. We have fought for too long time for a state of our own not to understand such a fight, when done by others. We know unfortunately better than many other nations what it means for a nation to have a state of its own. Our nation knows the gas chambers like the Jewish people did and our nation has not forgotten, like some others, the sad lesson of this war.

In our opinion we all have a common debt towards the nation which gave so much to the world and was so badly repaid, and it is now the moment to repay this thousand year-old debt.

Poland and the Land of Israel[1]

Some states, whose representatives are present here in this room, have asked why Poland, of all nations, why this new Poland, so actively supports the Jewish cause in Palestine, the partition of Palestine, the establishment in Palestine of a national sovereign Jewish state.

The present Polish government has always and still strives to explain to the United Nations all its political decisions. Those responsible for the implementation of Polish foreign policy have always endeavored to clarify and explain Poland's position so that it can be fully understood by international society. I am therefore especially keen to try and answer those questions relating to our position on the question of Palestine, to explain what it has always been and still is.

First, let me turn to our interest in Palestine in general. This interest is, in Poland, despite its geographical distance, very lively and takes many forms. For the Polish nation, Catholic in its overwhelming majority, where the traditions of faith and national identity are closely linked, this land is for us—just as it is for many nations represented in this assembly—the Holy Land, swathed in all the glory of Christendom. In addition, it is a land closely linked to the Arab world, the world of the Islamic Orient; and although we have in the past been involved in military conflict with this world, these battles have not poisoned later relations between our nations, just as the old Anglo-French antagonism does not darken current relations between France and Great Britain.

---

1   Speech by Ksawery Pruszyński, Polish delegate and chairman of Subcommittee One of the United Nations' Ad Hoc Committee on the Question of Palestine, delivered in Flushing Meadows before the General Assembly vote on Resolution 181 on November 29, 1947. In the Polish original, Pruszyński used the Hebrew word *erec*—*eretz* in the English transliteration. (Transl.)

From history we remember now not so much the wars we fought against each other, but more the period which at the end of the eighteenth century began the process of twilight and eclipse for Poland and for the world of Islam, the time of decline and bondage.

The struggle for national independence and sovereignty, which many Arab nations have fought, or are still fighting, against the colonial powers, has always found the warmest feeling of sympathy among Poles—and in Polish foreign policy, many, even quite recently, material manifestations of active support.

We are genuinely pleased to see representatives from Syria, Lebanon, Egypt, Pakistan, and Saudi Arabia, Iran and Yemen in this international forum,[2] and we welcome the entry of representatives of other ancient Arab nations into international life. The more so since we can now hear them speak with the voice of their own nations and not that of foreign powers. It is in this same spirit that we have tried, as far as possible, not to divide Palestine in such a way that the borders drawn up now will become insurmountable walls in the future. This is why we have supported the most recent, seemingly hopeless, attempts to reach a direct understanding between Arabs and Jews. This is why in our plan of partition we have tried to draw up borders, infrastructural links, and interconnections, so that a future agreement between the two sides, perhaps still far off, but which never should be ruled out, will discover more bridges than obstacles.

Yet it is also true that Poland has a particular Jewish interest in Palestine. This issue has been raised by some Arab representatives here, but—in my view—they have missed the point. So please allow me now to set it straight.

Yes, Poland has a historical interest in supporting the creation of a Jewish state in Palestine—this is true. However, the reasons for this interest are altogether different from those assumed by these Arab representatives. They are wrong to think that Poland views a Jewish state in Palestine as a kind of reservoir into which it can channel its own "inconvenient" Jewish population. I understand why they might think that. First, they assume that Poland in 1947 is still the same the Poland of 1939, and secondly that the country still has its large Jewish minority. However, between 1939 and 1947 the largest war in human history took place there, and with all its deadly weight. The overwhelming majority of the Jewish population of Poland has been murdered; the small fraction that has survived is, by the force of circumstances, being assimilated. Antisemitism, which unfortunately also survived, thus outliving those it was

---

2   Of course, Iran and Pakistan are not Arab states. (Author)

originally meant to harm, is actively fought by the Polish government today in a way rarely seen in history, and never before in Poland.

However, perhaps it is precisely because of that antisemitism, and the sense of guilt for our sins in the past, that the Jewish cause lies so near our heart. My nation was the closest living witness of the terrifying mass murder carried out by Germany on the Jews; my country was the place of those executions—and this is why the fate of the Jews has shaken us to the core. It is that past, and that fate, which has stirred in us this conviction that a nation for centuries deprived of its motherland has to have a motherland to return to, that it has to find its HOME.[3] In our view the Jewish nation is the most tragic nation in the world. And it is also the nation, in my view, to whom the world owes the most.

It is to the Jews that we owe the idea of the One God—Judaism is the root of Christianity. The holy books of this nation constitute that source from which the world's nations have drawn more than from any other vessel of human thought. This nation has given us an example how a small nation ought to—and can—resist the violence of the stronger, how David defeated Goliath, how the Maccabees went to their death. It was their poetry that sounded for the first time—and loudly—the note of longing for the land of forefathers, sung over the rivers of Babylon.

In their Diaspora, they have shown an invincible will to survive; from within their midst, people who have served the whole of humanity, like Spinoza and Heine, Mendelssohn and Marx, have emerged. All of us in this room, including those from the Arab nations, are in debt—yes, in debt—to this pauper who has now claimed his rights to the land from which he was banished by force. Shall we send him back with nothing?

Gentlemen, you are right to claim that in this whole matter Poland has demonstrated more concern that other nations about the fate of Israel. We accept these—presumably sarcastic—words as the highest praise for our foreign policy. This is the case. We have defended the cause of the Spanish people; we have, and will, defend freedom of the Greeks; and we support Indonesia in its fight for independence. We have defended, and will always defend, any just cause, which is why we have been defending, and will defend, the Jewish cause. We are defending it because of all those thousands of threads that bind us to those Jewish people who came looking for refuge in medieval Poland—even then, in the Middle Ages, fleeing persecution from Germany. We are defending

---

3   A phrase taken from the 1917 text of the Balfour Declaration, which discussed creating a Jewish "National HOME" in Palestine. (Author)

it now for we feel humbled by the guilt of the weighty sins we committed against this nation in the sad, and still not so distant, past.

But there is yet another reason why we defend it. No other nation understands better than the Polish nation the longing for one's own land, the land that belonged to one's ancestors, where one should not have to suffer the fate of an intruder or pilgrim. This is the reason why the Polish nation understands the struggle of Palestinian Jewry. The right each nation has to sovereign existence on the land of its ancestors—that is the international rule supported by the Polish nation. Independence, the right to one's own national state—this is a need which we Poles understand perhaps better than others, which is why today we understand the demands and aspirations of the Jews in Palestine and beyond, just as we understand every thirst for freedom, every struggle for freedom.

Photographs

New Jerusalem: on the way to the bazaar

Photo: Ksawery Pruszyński

New Jerusalem: The Hebrew University.

Photo: Ksawery Pruszyński

New Jerusalem: The Bezalel School of Arts and Crafts

Photo: Ksawery Pruszyński

New Jerusalem: sport exercises in Beth Hakarem

Photo: Ksawery Pruszyński

Kibbutz 1932

Photo: Anon, from: "Mojżesz i Ksawery", Twój Styl, Warszawa, 1999

Mojżesz Pomeranz and Ksawery Pruszyński in Kraków in the 1930s

Photo: Anon, from: "Mojżesz i Ksawery", Twój Styl, Warszawa, 1999

Mojżesz Pomeranz in Tel Aviv in 1948

Photo: Anon, from: "Mojżesz i Ksawery", Twój Styl, Warszawa, 1999

Ksawery and Mieczysław Pruszyński in Palestine 1942

Photo: Anon, from: "Mojżesz i Ksawery", Twój Styl, Warszawa, 1999

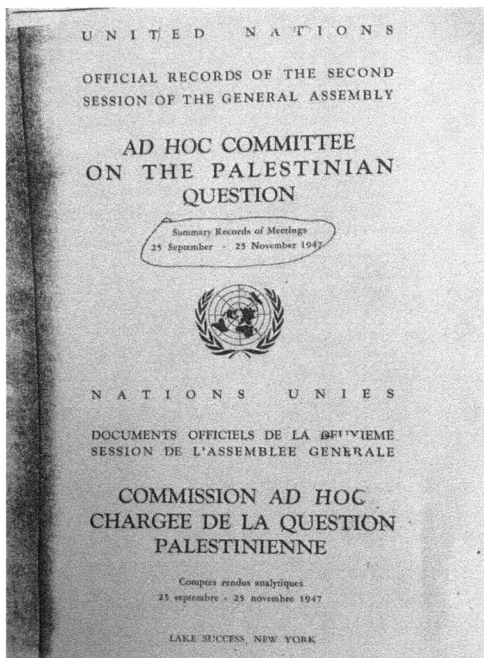

Summary records of meetings 25.09-25.11.1947; un official records of the second session of the General Assembly, Ad Hoc Committee on the question of Palestinian Question, Lake Success, New York

Photo: Anon, from: "Mojżesz i Ksawery", Twój Styl, Warszawa, 1999

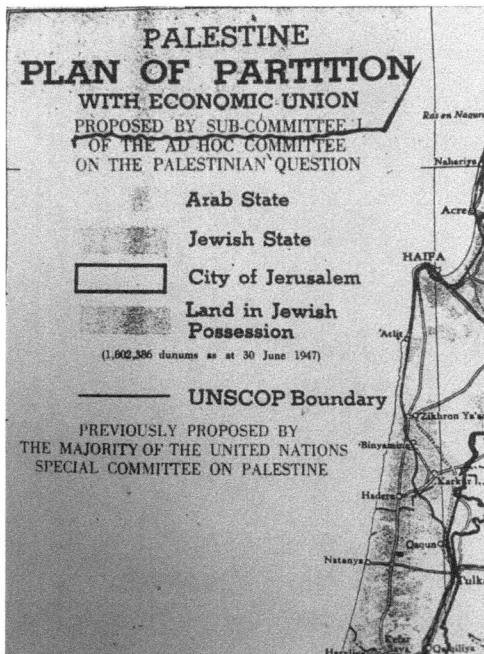

Palestine: Plann of Partition, proposal submitted by Subcommittee One, chaired by Ksawery Pruszyński

Photo: Wiesiek Powaga, 2019; The Pruszyński Family Archives

Manuscript of Ksawery Pruszyński's speech delivered on 25 November 1947 at the final session of the Ad Hoc Committee, un temporary headquarters, Flushing Meadows, New York

Photo: Wiesiek Powaga, 2019;
The Pruszyński Family Archivesw

Telegram with congratulation and thanks sent to Ksawery Pruszyński by the chairman of the General Council of Jewish Community in Palestine, one of many received by Ksawery Pruszyński in the wake of the historic vote on Tthe 29 November 1947

Photo: Wiesiek Powaga, 2019; The Pruszyński Family Archives

ing Solomon's Temple and Tabernacle

—IN—
—Library—

דער אידישער מורה דרך, וועג-וויזער
Der Yiddisher Moreh Derech, Veg-Veiser

CENTER of JEWISH GUIDE, Inc.
156 HENRY STREET   NEW YORK CITY
Phone ORchard 4-2215

ספרית

ב"ה

December 4, 1947

Hon. Xavery Pruschinsky
Chairman, UN SUB-COMM.1 on PALESTINE
Polish Delegation Quarters
151 East 57 Street
New York City

Hon. Sir:

We thank you sincerely for your kind acceptance of
our invitation to be the Guest of Honor at our Exhi-
bition of the models of the Tabernacle, King Solomon's
Holy Temple and other fragments of the Holy Land on
Tuesday, Dec.9,1:30 PM.at our new building, 152-154
Henry Street, New York City, and celebration of the
UN pronouncement of a Jewish State in Palestine.

Looking forward to greeting your Excellency within
our walls and to enjoying the oratory of your eloquent
address, we remain,

Respectfully yours,

HOUSE OF SAGES, Inc.

Rabbi Samuel A. Rubin
The Jewish Guide
Executive Director

*Invitation for a celebration of the "Un Pronouncement of a Jewish State in Palestine" sent by
Rabbi Samuel Rubin, Chairman of the Jewish Guide in New York, dated 4 December 1947*

Photo: Wiesiek Powaga, 2019; The Pruszyński Family Archives

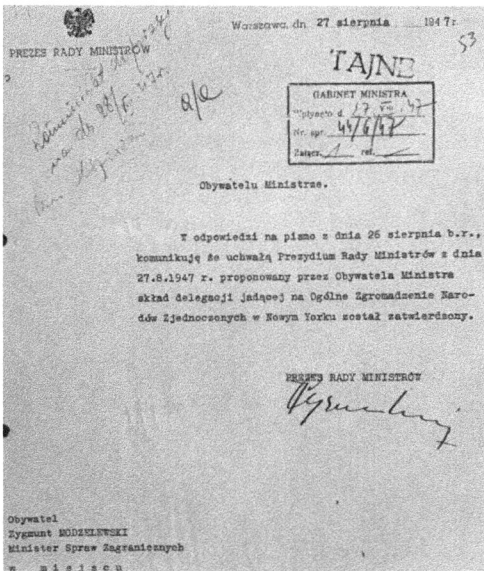

Document of the Polish Foreign Office confirming the list of Polish delegation sent to the UN General Assembly, Signed by the Prime Minister Józef Cyrankiewicz

Photo: Wiesiek Powaga, 2019;
The Pruszyński Family Archives

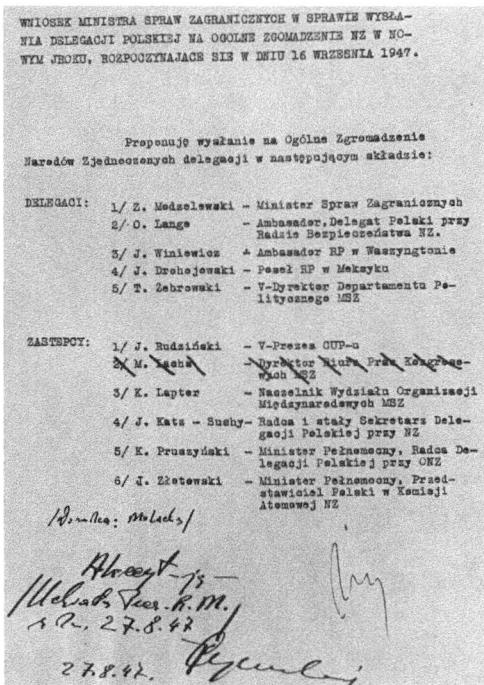

PREZES RADY MINISTRÓW

Warszawa, dn. 27 sierpnia 1947 r.

TAJNE

GABINET MINISTRA

wpłynęło d. ....
Nr. spr. 4476/...
Załącz. .... ref. ....

Obywatelu Ministrze.

W odpowiedzi na pismo z dnia 26 sierpnia b.r., komunikuję że uchwałą Prezydium Rady Ministrów z dnia 27.8.1947 r. proponowany przez Obywatela Ministra skład delegacji jadącej na Ogólne Zgromadzenie Narodów Zjednoczonych w Nowym Yorku został zatwierdsony.

PREZES RADY MINISTRÓW

Obywatel
Zygmunt MODZELEWSKI
Minister Spraw Zagranicznych
w miejscu.

WNIOSEK MINISTRA SPRAW ZAGRANICZNYCH W SPRAWIE WYSŁA-
NIA DELEGACJI POLSKIEJ NA OGÓLNE ZGOMADZENIE NZ W NO-
WYM JROKU, ROZPOCZYNAJĄCE SIĘ W DNIU 16 WRZEŚNIA 1947.

Proponuję wysłanie na Ogólne Zgromadzenie Narodów Zjednoczonych delegacji w następującym składzie:

DELEGACI:
1/ Z. Modzelewski — Minister Spraw Zagranicznych
2/ O. Lange — Ambasador, Delegat Polski przy Radzie Bezpieczeństwa NZ.
3/ J. Winiewicz — Ambasador RP w Waszyngtonie
4/ J. Drohojewski — Poseł RP w Meksyku
5/ T. Żebrowski — V-Dyrektor Departamentu Politycznego MSZ

ZASTĘPCY:
1/ J. Rudziński — V-Prezes GUP-u
2/ M. Lachs — Dyrektor Biura Prac Kongresowych MSZ
3/ K. Lapter — Naczelnik Wydziału Organizacji Międzynarodowych MSZ
4/ J. Katz - Suchy — Radca i stały Sekretarz Delegacji Polskiej przy NZ
5/ K. Pruszyński — Minister Pełnomocny, Radca Delegacji Polskiej przy ONZ
6/ J. Żółtowski — Minister Pełnomocny, Przedstawiciel Polski w Komisji Atomowej NZ

List Mojżesza Pomeranza z Jerozolimy do Ksawerego Pruszyńskiego w Nowym Jorku, datowany 28 listopada 1947 r.

Copy of the letter sent by Mojżesz Pomeranz to Ksawery Pruszyński on the eve of the UN vote on Resolution 181, dated 28 November 1947

Photo: Wiesiek Powaga, 2019; The Pruszyński Family Archives

Second session of the United Nations General Assembly opens in Flushing Meadows, 16 September 1947, United Nations (Flushing Meadows), New York. Items on the 63-point agenda include the Palestine Question. Ksawery Pruszyński 5th in the right bottom row

Photo: UN Photo Library, #86350

Ad Hoc Committee on the Palestine Question of the United Nations General Assembly (Lake Success, New York, 22 November 1947. View of the 26th meeting of the 57-member Ad Hoc Committee on the Palestinian Question. Ksawery Pruszyński 3rd from the left, top left corner

Dr. Herbert V. Evatt, Australia, Chairman of the Ad Hoc Committee talks with Ksawery Pruszyński before the first meeting of Sub-Committees 1. Pruszyński was later elected Chairman of Sub-Committees 1 which was established to draw up a detailed plan for the future government of Palestine in accordance with the recommendations and majority plan of the United Nations Special Committee on Palestine (UNSCOP)

First meeting of oSub-Committees 1 of the United Nations Ad Hoc Committee on the Palestinian Question. At table, left to right, are: Ksawery Pruszyński, Poland, elected Chairman of Sub-Committees 1 during first meeting; Jorge Garcia-Granados, Guatemala Delegation Chairman; Karel Lisicky, Czechoslovakia

Professor Enrique Rodríguez Fabregat, right, permanent representative of Uruguay to the United Nations, and Dr. Enrique V. Corominas, Vice-Chairman of the delegation of Argentina to the Second Session of the United Nations General Assembly, discuss map of Partition Plan for Palestine, in conference room before 30th meeting of the Assembly's Ad Hoc Committee on the Palestinian Question

Members of the Jewish Agency delegation study a map of proposed partition of Palestine at
United Nations interim headquarters at Flushing Meadows, New York, 12 November 1947.
Left to right are: Dr. Nahum Goldmann, David Horovitz, Emanuel Neumann and Rabbi Wolf Gold.
United Nations

Index

www.ingramcontent.com/pod-product-compliance
Lightning Source LLC
Chambersburg PA
CBHW050651270326
41927CB00012B/2968